Bathing I

Bolcán na Sióga

A guide to relaxing in the forests

Allowing ourselves time to stop
and smell the forest for awhile

Inside here are stories and poems of
mythology, fairy stories and divine questions

also included ...

Ogma's Tale Of The Trees

a story of the creation of
the Ogham Alphabet
from the Memory of Trees

written by
Woodland Bard

published by
Bards In The Woods

published in 2015 by
Bards In The Woods Media
Carrowcrory Cottage, Ballinafad,
Co. Sligo, Ireland
bardsinthewoods.com

first edition

ISBN :1512253049

© John Willmott aka Woodland Bard 2015
who asserts all rights to be identified as author of
this work of Bathing In The Fae's Breath

All rights reserved

No part of this publication may be reproduced, distributed or transmitted in any form or by any means, including photocopying, recording, or other electronic or mechanical methods, without the prior written permission of the publisher, except in the case of brief quotations embodied in critical reviews and certain other noncommercial uses permitted by copyright law. For permission requests, write to the publisher, addressed "Attention: Permissions Coordinator," at the address below.

Now to enjoy the book.

I have broken tradition and have placed 'Acknowledgements' as 'Dedications' at the end.

So, here we go starting with Contents,
then into Introduction ...

Contents :

Introduction	5
... The Fae?	7
... Why I wrote this Book	9
... Maybe, I will Spin A Yarn	11
... The search for 'tumuli'	13
... What on Earth happened here?	16
... Another View Over Atlantis	18
... Genocide of Nature	21
... I watched Nature Dance	23
... Recovery	25
... Connecting with our Ancestors?	26
Do The Trees Call You	29
The Fae's Breath	34
When We Become A Tree	40
Purpose Of Poetry	43
Accept The Apple	47
... Did Adam eat an Apple?	50
... How did Apples spread?	54
... Avalon	55
... An Apple A Day ...	58
... Bless the Apple Trees	64
Why Do Trees Whisper	68
... Mother Trees	76
Who's Woods Are These?	79
The Handsome Frog	81
Song Of Airmid	99
... Deeds of the Tuatha De Dannan	99
... The Rage of Diancecht	101
... Airmid's Cloak	104
... Airmid of the Fae	107

Ogma's Tale Of The Trees ...

Introducing Ogma	114
Beith the Birch	121
Luis the Rowan	128
Fearn the Alder	141
Saille the Willow	148
Nuin the Ash	153
Huathe the Hawthorn	159
Duir the Oak	165
Tinne the Holly	173
Coll the Hazel	179
Quirt the Apple	185
Muin the Vine	191
Gort the Ivy	196
nGetal the Reed	202
Straif the Blackthorn	206
Ruis the Elder	211
Ailim the Pine	216
Ohn the Gorse	225
Ur the Heather	228
Eida the Poplar	235
Ioho the Yew	241

Invitations ...

Find Your Story	257
Be A Bard In The Woods	267
Sleeping Awake	274
Encore	276
Dedications	281

Introduction :

I started to compile this 'Bathing In The Fae's Breath' collection to respond to how we long for and desire to 'escape' into Nature.

Do we find ourselves longing to escape into Nature, to relax, relieve anxiety for awhile, maybe share a picnic, and then we leave again.

Not so long ago, Nature was where our ancestors resided and survived from. Today with our organized 'systems' of farming, manufacturing, distribution, and communications many of us seem to have been culturally and emotionally detached from 'our forests' and wild nature.

Do you discover that entering forests, along with coasts, mountains, prairies and wetlands, are still our best sanctuaries for relief, for nourishment, and for any needed sense of well being and healing?

As our lives do not seem to be dedicated to living the instincts, inspiration, and even Divinity, served by the realm of Nature any more, do we feel separated?

As I read back at what I have written in this book, I have discovered my work here is a quest to wander through a link between forests and fairy stories.

I also question how both forests and fairy stories seem to be at risk. To me, both the stories and native woodlands are fragile and have some concerning risk of possible extinction.

In Ireland, there is a saying that a squirrel could once travel from Dublin to Sligo without touching the ground, but not anymore.

Does the disappearing of both woodlands and fairy stories deprive us of our cultural flow? Like the squirrel who can no longer travel from Dublin to Sligo, do we find it difficult to find somewhere to engage in imaginative discovery?

Introduction

The Fae? ...

You may also wonder about the word, 'Fae' that I use in my book title here?

This is a word I have learned from what is now Scottish tradition. In Ireland, people talk more about the 'Fairies'. When they do, they seem to be speaking about a culture of 'little people' seen and unseen.

Within this book, I do not speak of fairies or the 'Fae', as being sweet little beings with wings. In the mythology I share with you here, the 'Fae' is the unseen ebbing and flowing of a Presence that orchestrates all the diversity of Nature through all weathers and cycles of seasons.

If we pause in an open space of Nature, especially within a forest, we may sense, imagine, and believe, that the 'Fae' are all dancing around us.

It may seem like some weaving work is happening around us through the busy-ness of several mysterious, maybe mischievous, unseen beings. These are the same invisible beings that have helped to keep bards and storytellers in work for 100s, maybe 1000s, of years.

You may know excellent teachers that describe their work in the woods as facilitating Forest Bathing, Forest Mindfulness, and Forest Therapy. I interpret what they offer as encouragement to go 'Bathing In The Fae's Breath'.

This is how I interpret
the beautiful romantic Gaelic phrase, ...
'Boladh na Sióga (bowa na sheega)'.

So here I have lured you into my interpretation of, 'Bathing In The Fae's Breath'. I trust you will enjoy the contents here and, especially, its encouragement to let the 'Fae's Breath' within the forests dissolve all that obstructs our senses.

By doing so, I have discovered we become
free and Present.

Nature changes from being a place to escape to. It becomes a place of Presence that heals, inspires, and motivates us. We begin to recognize Nature as being what we are always part of, and not as something to control, avoid, or sometimes visit.

Introduction

Why I wrote this book ...

May I indulge you into a story that motivated me to compile this book?

'Bathing In The Fae's Breath' started during a stroke that seized me during the wee hours of 6th May 2010. At that time, I did not think it was a stroke but thought it was a heart attack!

I rushed outside, gathered some Hawthorn tree leaves, blossoms, and some berries still hanging there from the year before. In the kitchen, I managed to switch on the kettle and pour the boiling water over all that I had gathered from a Hawthorn tree, all placed into a china teapot.

By now I was shaking and finding it hard to stand, but I still had the strength to pour myself a cup of this steaming sweet perfumed brew.

I returned to my bedroom, sat down and sipped the brew. I seemed to relax almost immediately and enjoyed a caressing intimate warming sensation, as we do from a good cup of tea.

That comforting warmth then turned into an unsettling cooling. I shivered more and more.

I became drowned with fear, thinking, oh no, this Hawthorn tea was not a good idea. The shivering stopped, but I could not move my legs, my arms, my neck, or anything through all my body. All I could do was take one more breath and no more

... and then I floated away and I briefly saw myself laying there.

Everything around me quickly melted away, no walls, no cottage, no form at all. I was thrust into a light like that moment of sunlight in your eyes.

Then, that light slowed down and rested into a kaleidoscope of colours that had no form except for a faded human shape that emerged from this multicoloured pool. This being, that instinct told me was a woman, was about to be my guide.

This guide was to show me a way. I surrendered to this immediately. I had no interest in seeing the guide's face, only to see what I was to be shown.

At this point I'm floundering here, seeking for the words to write down a description of what happened next. We seem to have no words in our language to truly share what happened. If I tried to, I would be stuck into duplicating worn clichés that I have remembered from movies.

Introduction

Maybe I will spin a yarn ...

The best I can offer you is to continue this now as a storyteller with a yarn.

There's no 'Once upon a time ...' here.
More fitting is 'how the Bards relate ...'

In a strange land long ago, that I thought I had forgotten, there I was as a very young boy just starting school. I was already a very good reader then, but I was bored with school from the moment I started going there.

The most tedious time was waiting for the others children to learn to read "Come John, Come". Yes, that is indeed the first reading lesson sentence in the first Janet and John book that all school children learned to read with back then.

By the time I had started going to primary school, I had almost read the entire Old Testament from the King James Bible. Through this, I had grasped the vision of stories, but not grasped what the Christian religion was about.

On a shelf in the two-roomed country school I attended, I saw a dusty Ordnance Survey map left on a window sill beside the library shelves.

I unfolded this map, with wonder, also wondering if I would be able to re-fold it again. Fully open, instantly I saw it's magic beckon me!

There were all of these colours, wavy contour lines, and mysterious symbols. I quickly learned these symbols showed where post offices were, churches, other schools and I wondered what this strange thing called 'tumuli' was. This was what I had to find out!

That following Friday, the map was still on the window sill, so I tucked it into my pullover and sneaked it out of school, took it home and hid it.

On Saturday, as was the routine then, I was pulled out of bed early, often before light, dragged to the bus stop, onto the bus and off to market and do other Saturday morning shopping routines. Following this was the ritual of stodgy food and custard lunch, then home on the afternoon bus and ordered to do my chores before dark ... but Sunday was different. It was always my day off.

In those days, in the country, a child had freedom to go off and play all day. Well, I did have time to wander as I was not forced off to 'church' like other family children were.

Introduction

The search for 'tumuli' ...

So for me, I grabbed some bread and cheese from the bread bin and air cooled larder hole in the wall, and off I peddled on my wee 18 inch wheel bike saying I will be back in time for Sunday dinner, that we call 'lunch' today, at around 3 pm. I was now free to discover what a 'tumuli' was!

Actually, it was not far away, outside the next village, maybe just two miles away. This 'tumuli' was on farmland. As I had been taught some manners, I went up to the farmhouse, knocked on a door, and surprised the farmer's wife by seeming to be like some begging urchin.

She hastened to get her farmer husband, to 'deal' with me before I could say much.

As he bent over towards me with puffing pipe and scowl, I asked him,
"Please Mister, can I have a look at your 'tumuli'?

He bellow laughed and said,
"Why do you wanna see those ol' stanes fer?".

I replied, making it up quickly,
"I hear that fairies can be seen dancing there at Spring Equinox".

I think he was taken aback by me knowing what Spring Equinox is, but he replied ...
"Now you mention that, my mother used to say ..... my father used to say ....".

Stories kept flowing from him as he walked with me over to those "ol' stanes".

Those 'stanes' happened to be just a couple of them set in the ground like a couple of well-worn and poorly formed grave headstones.

I knew, then, it was not the stones I had come to see, but to hear the stories, look at the landscape around me, then put the two together to understand why those "ol' stanes" were there. I have learned, since then, that no archeology book or history book can ever do that.

For about 53 years and 8 months after that first encounter with a 'tumuli', I carried fascination and wonder to 100s, maybe 1000s, of ancient megalithic sites that I visited.

Yes, 100s of places like Stonehenge, Avebury, Newgrange, Callanish and many others places of ordered stones described as ...
'older than the pyramids'.

Introduction

I discovered that Ordnance Survey maps also labeled stone circles, standing stones, cairns, henges, and wells. Not all of them were 'tumuli'.

Some stone and henge sites were not even marked, but I learned to read contours, wall shapes and ring symbols that indicated more sites were present.

At all of these ancient sites, I questioned their possible metaphysical connections and manifestations.

More than that, I carried my ultimate question ... "What on earth happened here?" ...

What on earth happened here? ...

That 'question' was explored by me through many years through folk drama and theatrics that I urged friends to join me with, while they lasted.

Strangely, my friends have more memories of those times than I do. I was compulsively composing and expressing through cacophonous performances of songs, poetry, stories and musicky compositions. I still do that today.

I think I will end that story there for now, so I can tell more in future books I write.

So these were the memories my Divine guide was passing me through again, but with a very different interpretation.

So, what about the Ley Lines?

Surely they should be in my story about my adventures of visiting ancient megalithic sites?

Oh yes, they are, and what a journey the wonder of ley lines can lead us into. Ley lines, the human dream of feng shui of the landscape that we should honour, support and enhance?

Introduction

So there was I, wandering, for several years, with my Jack The Lad 'Old Straight Track' LP under one arm, while reciting from my John Michell 'View Over Atlantis' book held by one hand, while also trying to dangle a gold ring, tied to one of my long hairs, with the other hand, over an Ordnance Survey map, and all this with expectations of achieving some magical dowsing revelation.

And then through the curse of this paralytic stroke I had been struck with, and this Divine guide appearing, a kind of angel of "I told you so, but you would never listen", who had wrenched my 'spirit' from my body to take me on a timeless, spaceless walkabout that seem to last for months.

This whole experience was probably no more than two minutes in human time

... and here is the different interpretation I was shown on that 'timeless' journey.

Another View Over Atlantis ...

I was reminded that stone circles, stone cairns, stone courts, stone dolmens, stone henges, stone standing stones, and stone crosses are all creations from humans hands binding together stones they had ripped from our planet.

All of these are stones that can never return to the planet' fabric in the same way again. As guests on this earth, we have re-arranged the furniture, that the planet provided for us, in a way that we cannot leave the way we found it.

Each of these constructions, by humans, were and are of human design and human command by one or few people. Today we may describe these people as being the '1%', who ordered the other '99%' to build these structures in return for minimal accommodation and food.

Yes, there are stories told of these places also being built by seemingly leaderless communities of desirable equality who lived a bit like organised ants or murmuring starlings. This 'spiritual' guided tour, I was on, did not reveal that, though.

My 'Divine' guide showed me how the '99%' majority of humans became enslaved to the '1%'.

Introduction

This '1%' being no different to corporate board members, government cabinets, dictator commanders, royal family members, and religious leaders and their guards that we have 'ruling' us around the planet at present.

The one difference we create in our minds, hearts and souls is to vision these ancient 'elite' equivalents as being heroes, Divine teachers, and even gods and goddesses with a gifted earthly presence. I was shown how this reverence towards these 'select elite' humans displaced a 'Presence Of Love' within the '99%', which is really most of us human beings.

Going away from this Divine guided tour, I am sharing here, I am now reminded of something someone said to me ...

"I once heard that human leaders are not the prophets. Leaders are the people who dared to take ownership of words that un-named prophets once said and created industries and trade around them, after selling those words to us to believe in".

"Slavery is when we give away our Presence Of Love to the 'Power inventory' of another".

What about the Ley Lines wisdom that I had developed an 'unbreakable' belief in?

My guide showed me ley lines as being the plotting of the 'human dream' for order and attempting to control the flow of nature. I feared my guide's was revealing these as being an attempted enslavement of all life.

My guide reminded me that Nature had its own flow, like the flow of the realm I was in through this Divine tour. I was shown that both are the same except one is seen, and the other is unseen.

I could feel the 'Presence Of Love', flow freely through both realms together without order, without any mathematical geometrical calculation.

The nearest we may get to understand this is through the computation of Pi, the calculation of the ratio of the circumference of a circle to its diameter. The result is infinite, never ending. This seems to relate our human linear thinking in relation to the spherical, almost cycle, moving flow of Nature.

Introduction

Genocide of Nature ...

My Divine guided tour then took me through the human genocide of Nature.

I was shown how each human construction created from stone clears away webs of interacting life to make each construction possible.

I was shown how each walled or fenced field is an attempted genocide clearing all other life present to make human food farming possible.

No longer can the human race trust food to be provided by Nature. No longer can a squirrel travel from Dublin to Sligo without touching the ground, and maybe starve too.

I was shown how humans had constructed buildings with a belief that they connect us to the singular Divine. Buildings detached from earthly biodiversity of Nature, pointing with spires and towers towards an unknown in the universe.

Over centuries, we have accepted all of these changes and our new beliefs became moulded. Our beliefs changed from faith in what is around us to a belief that there is always somewhere much better than where we ever are.

Religions teach us that we must work to earn the gift of being in that 'better place', that some describe as 'Heaven'.

Some people reading this now may feel, may fear, that where I was guided from through those few minutes was a realm of 'Hell', and my guide was actually 'Satan', so some may say. But it was from there I was shown a sort of 'hell' that we humans have chosen to create to live in.

We have our houses, cottages, mansions and apartments, all built through a process of clearing away all other life that was once living and was home for them in those spaces.

We arrange our gardens to control what is present there, deciding what should be planted where, ... and anything not within our design is a 'weed'.

I was shown the stress that maintaining this human order can give us.

Introduction

I watched Nature dance ...

Birds were dropping seeds, animals transporting seeds. None of them seemed to be aware about how their simple actions create new life. I watched these seeds becoming trees, and around them more trees grew to form forests.

I was shown the water of clouds falling, sinking through the soil, finding pathways to flow through the rocks, and ways to flow to the surface again as springs of clean, nutritious water. Water that is full of nutritious minerals collected during their flow that could heal and nourish us.

None of this is planned, yet moment by moment all of these seemingly spontaneous actions were responding to that unseen conductor of life.
This is Nature.

When an elegant tree grows from a seed unplanned; When clean pure water flows from the earth undesigned.

Are not these the 'sacred places' to us?

Are these not more sacred than anything we could construct ourselves?

Understanding this is when we realize that, we are 'Bathing In The Fae's Breath'.

We are in the Presence Of Love, and that we are in the earthly equivalent of where I was for those few moments with my Divine guide.

My time with my guide was done. I looked up, and I saw the face of an ambulance man ...

Introduction

Recovery ...

I did recover from that stroke, and I'm ok now, except my spirit is very different.

I still live in a beautiful cottage, and still 'organize' and keep a Tree Labyrinth garden, but that today has become quite a diverse permaculture paradise without me trying.

Now, I express what I was shown and learned through those timeless couple of minutes, perhaps comparable to that extended orgasm we all long to experience.

Now, I express what I can of those few moments, how I can, through stories, poetry, songs, music, drama, and sometimes a wee dance.

I express the visions of those moments through sorrow, joy (I love a joke or two), and dreaming as there is always dark, light, and that vortex place and space between.

Connecting with Ancestors ...

Is it worth it? ...

Yes, I do still visit those ancient stone circles, cairns, dolmens and 'monuments' like I have done passionately for most of my life.

Also, 100s of thousands of people do come to Ireland to see these relics of ancient times much more than coming here for the living. So I still share these places with visitors that ask me to.

For many people, these quiet still ruined places of their ancestors somehow provides a connection to a heritage they feel they and their family ancestors was forced away from.

They may blame the English, cruel rich landlords, famines, Queen Victoria, Cromwell, the Normans, sometimes the Vikings.

Often they leave Ireland in tears. Glad to have had the opportunity to be where their ancestors once were, and to connect to those places again ...

But within them, there is still a longing present.

Introduction

At these ancient megalithic sites, that many still call 'Sacred' with a capital 'S', I no longer share the stones with praises of the 'gods and goddesses' in the stories linked to them like I used to.

I now visit these ancient places to celebrate the algae, mosses, fungi, grasses, flowers, shrubs and trees that have found their way to these places.

I celebrate how they are now free again to spread and share their dance of biodiversity as best they can around these stones. The bees find abundance around them once more, too.

I visit these ancient places to celebrate the return of the 'Fae' again. 'Fae Presence' is there through all living things that have become abundant again.

I honour Trees and water gifts from the earth that have found their way back

This is what I do now, once John Willmott the Ley Hunter, and now I'm the Woodland Bard.

So please enjoy my 'Bathing In The Fae's Breath' collection, here in this book.

Bathing In The Fae's Breath

Before you do, as I finished writing this long introduction, a poet friend Edward Durand posted on Facebook a quote by writer George Russell, who said of Eva Gore-Booth of Sligo,...

"I feel you belong to the spiritual clan of new Irish people... who know that Tir na n'Og is no dream and that inwardly we are inhabitants of it and breathe a common air."

Do The Trees Call You?

Do The Trees Call You? :

Where is that place where we can go
to feel free to follow what speaks to us
through our inner voice.?

Where is that sacred place
where inspiration is our guide,
or where our guide speaks to us,
and says its ok to switch on the light,
to become present with our 'Holy Grail' Chalice,
brimming with all that we yearn to
see, touch, smell, resonate and drink from?

For me, what I have discovered, seemingly a long, long time ago, is how important it is to be able to return to one of Nature's native woodlands at least once a week to be part of its diverse union. This is always uplifting, no matter what the weather is.

Such a woodland has to be native, a woodland that looks after itself, and be a space for the diversity of what we call 'Nature' that may have lived here, a home here, before time began.

Such a woodland, I always find, lets my inner voice, the inner calling, speak quietly and trusted. I hope you find a woodland that is a place where you can surrender your whole being like that too.

Our woodland inspirations may serve us questions. Questions that we respond to, perhaps when we feel anxious, and perhaps feeling powerless to forage, find or cultivate answers to.

If, we call upon courage, or maybe we just need patience, to live with our questions rather than seek to find answers, we find ourselves revelling on the journey that our questions inspire us to follow. We discover this is 'living'. We discover this IS what we have been 'longing' for.

Do The Trees Call You?

I am a keeper of a Tree Labyrinth in rural Co. Sligo, Ireland. It was created and planted according to a stream of repeated dreams I had.

Now, many people visit our
Tree Labyrinth at Carrowcrory.

They listen to my introduction, stroll the labyrinth without me present, and at their speed ... and they discover that their 'intuition' volume increases, as they walk it's path.

Do you have a chosen place, which you have discovered, where you find yourself opening to this beautiful flow of Divine inspiration without effort?

Many people also join us for Bards In The Woods within local public access forests.

We meet up on Sunday afternoons, go on a stroll, help each other identify trees and plants, engage in a quiet time, so our senses are touched and bonded with what is around us.

We share favourite poems and stories in a chosen location, often by water, then finish with a fellowship of fun through a shared picnic.

In conversation, during these Sunday afternoons, people present ask each other, if there is a 'tool', a 'special tool', a ritual, or even a Divine charm or chant, that can arouse our inspirations within the forests at any time.

We seek for 'inspirations' to enable us to make comfortable 'secure' decisions to manage our relationships, resources, and health.

Some people also wonder how they could be part of a local, national or even global 'medicine' that could actively heal and protect our challenged world, our challenged environment?

In the woods at a picnic table, or in our cottage after a labyrinth walk, visitors talk with each other while sharing tea, scones, and delights made from local foods.

These conversations often express longings for future days.

Our visitors describe their dreams of when our world could be full of people and cultures who respect the ebbs and flows of nature. I believe this is the quiet human dream of most of us.

While sharing our picnic, our food, we also talk about how our actions and consumptions can become more sustainable and more friendly for this earth.

Who of us collapses in bed at night, after a busy, productive day, and travel into a silent prayer?

Are these silent prayers responses to our wishes to be shown ways of how to be a better balance with all things living?

Are we shown how to be of better service to our land and the people around us?

When the morning light returns, sometimes before we rise, our visions are pure and revealing. As we physically awake and venture back into that 'tick-tock world' that is our routine our morning visions seem to fade. So this is why I ask ...

Do The Trees Call You?

It is among them where we can go
'Bathing In The Fae's Breath' ... so let's go :-)

The Fae's Breath :

When the Trees have called,
Will you go where they are?
If you go to the woods today.
Are you in for for a big surprise?

I will speak of Boladh na Síoga,
(bowa na shee ga),
Bathing in The Fae's Breath.
Japanese people call this Shinrin Yoku,
And the Koreans call this Sanlimyok

The Fae's Breath

So how is this done?
This Forest Bathing,
This Forest Mindfulness.
This Forest Wellness.

Go to a forest, take a deep breath;
Wander along curious trails there.
Many forests make this easy,
Where calm embraces us instantly.

Follow the trails,
Let your senses loose
from your baggage and shackles.
Smell the aromas of the trees, shrubs and flowers,
And the potency of the living earth itself.

Find water there and listen.
Let visions come to you from that water.
Touch the bark, leaves, flowers, and berries.
Forage and taste those that are safe,
nourishing and even healing.

This is not just Forest Bathing.
This is Bathing In The Faes Breath.

Its a return to a simple tradition,
Arousal of a suppressed instinct,
Moment of harmony with nature,
To join in with its song and dance.

Bathing In The Fae's Breath

Feel the forest welcome you,
Embracing you,
Connecting you,
Accepting your prayers,
And returning responses.

Science may speak of the benefits of this,
Composed within their laboratory temples.
Statistics of wellness unravel on our screens,
But being there needs no proving.

Sights, aromas, sounds, sensations, and tastes,
Bathe us completely;
Breathe on us gently;
Calming, healing and nourishment.

Even 15 minutes in a forest,
Allowing this gift,
Allowing this embrace,
Allowing this connection,

Can bathe us and soak into
Our entire being.
And its all simple,
All very, very simple.

Stress dissolves,
Blood pressure drops,
Mental clarity improves,

The Fae's Breath

Inner visions are remarkable.
This is not just a stroll through a forest,
But also time to sit awhile.
A time for quiet that we allow,
All else to shut down and switch off.

Never bring goals or schedules into a forest.
Trust instincts to wander
and have senses awaken.
Leave behind our linear ways,
And join the circles of cycles that is the forest.

When you sit quietly, notice how sounds change.
Activities of the forest change
As you become relaxed and connected,
So does everything around
becomes connected to you.

When you are with others in a forest,
Agree with each other for a time,
To refrain from all conversation,
But do allow a time to play.

Then gather together to share
Feelings, inspirations, and stories.
Use a talking stick to pass around,
So each has a voice to share
and an audience to hear

Bathing In The Fae's Breath

Create poems and prose
From your new visions.
Share those poems in the Woods.
Become Bards, Bards In The Woods.

Bring food and refreshment to share.
A picnic of fellowship together,
To celebrate life, love and connection,
And pride in where you are today.

When you are back home,
And through the days to follow,
Notice how something is very different,
In the ways you think, feel and do things.

Does this justify any effort,
To get outside for a little time.
To venture into a Forest,
To Bathe In The Fae's Breath again?

To be timeless;
To surrender your senses;
You are part of nature again.
Within whatever weather it chooses to serve.

So cross that bridge,
Cross that threshold,
Cross that veil, into the forest of ...

The Fae's Breath

Being connected,
Being loved,
Being a Bard,,
And encouraging others to be the same.

In the Shinrin Yoku tradition;
In the Sanlimyok tradition;
In the Boladh na Sióga tradition;
Bathing yourself in Fae's Breath of the Forest.

When We Become A Tree :

Why is it that we enter a forest
worn out, stressed, tired, uninspired,
and often don't want to 'waste' our time
is some darned forest? ...

When We Become A Tree

Eventually we leave the forest
feeling fresh, transformed, inspired,
happy, visionary, focused
and even brave,
but why do we need to leave?

See, hear, smell, touch and taste this tree
Be part of its wonderful spontaneous
ebb and flow dance
as one of its diverse guests
circling and swirling together
by a unifying unseen element.

I believe we can become a tree too
accepting, trusting, and dancing
within the unity in all things.

Through being a tree, as a tree
I am confident we restore peace,
and clarity within ourselves,
and that clarity links with all trees
all animals, all birds and all life

I feel that any tree,
is a dynamic creation, a moving fusion,
of static stillness and intense movement,
a spiral dance with no beginning or end.
inviting us to share the constant
flow and ebb of creativity

Bathing In The Fae's Breath

When we become a tree
we discover what we call the Divine,
we discover the unseen light,
we discover we have not created a language
to describe life, and accept we never will.

But we often call all this, She
a Universal Mother
and we give her names

I sometimes call out for the
Mór na Coire Ciúin, to lay with me
but it is the
Bri de Óg, that comes to me.
Fire from the Arrow, spark of lust, unity and birth
is the intensity that is thrust upon me.

But together, that intense movement I need,
and the still silence I crave.
dance together to preserve wholeness and infinity.

Let us not talk of time
and being somewhere else,
just lets be, be here, ,
which is what happens
when We Become A Tree.

Purpose Of Poetry

Purpose Of Poetry :

I will start with a Poem from the woods ...

Who Believes The Fae Are Here?

Who believes the Fae are here,
Within this tree, do we feel love or fear.
Can they carry our prayers past the moon
To unveil our dreams very soon? ...

Bathing In The Fae's Breath

Who believes that wonder
Brings us more gold than plunder;
Believes magic is the miracle of truth,
And not a potion for eternal youth?

Who believes songs of love
Are not blessings from above
Beyond vision, beyond view,
But of voices of those who watch over you?

These trees are quiet, where are the Fae?
A secret we will unlock today.
Nobody can tell us, nobody can speak,
When a fairy ring becomes the forest we seek.

If you believe in the Fae and always stay true,
They will always be present and watch over you.
So be kind to their trees.
Do not strangle them

… or nail in coins please!

Purpose Of Poetry

**Robin Williams as John Keaton
in the Dead Poet's Society movie said ...**

We don't read and write poetry
because it's cute.
We write poetry because
we are members of the human race.
And the human race
is filled with passion,
Poetry, beauty, romance, love.
These are what we stay alive for.
And you may contribute a verse.
What will your verse be?

Robert Frost talking about Poetry ...
coupled poetry and power,
because he saw poetry as the
means of saving power from itself ...

When power leads man toward arrogance,
poetry reminds him of his limitations.

When power narrows the areas of man's concern,
poetry reminds him of the richness
and diversity of his existence.

When power corrupts, poetry cleanses,
For art establishes the basic human truths which
must serve as the touchstone of our judgment.

Bathing In The Fae's Breath

I often think poetry is like a dog listening to a human speaking. Only a few words are understood by the dog, but by doing so the dog understands the whole message and conversation.

This short monologue speaks to me as poetry, as I regard poetry as being the voice of memory ...

"Something lives only as long
as the last person who remembers it.
I always trust memory over history.
Memory, like fire, is radiant,
while history serves only those
who seek to control it,
the people who douse the flame of memory
in order to put out the fire of truth.
Beware of these people
for they are dangerous and unwise.
Their false history is written in the blood
of those who may remember the truth."

-- from a speech by Floyd Westerman
as Albert Hosteen in The X-Files episode,
"The Blessing Way"

Accept The Apple :

Apple as a Tree Of Life ...

Let's step back to our so-called 'origin', the Tree of Life or World Tree, often known as Yggrasil from Norse mythology.

The mythology of this tree is that it was somehow involved in the creation of the universe, the origin of humanity, and the Divine gifts of nourishment.

Some say this sacred tree was an Ash tree, and Norse tradition seems to say so, Some say this sacred tree was an Oak, as told in Celtic tales.

A few Celtic tales speak of this tree being an Elm, and some say this tree was a Birch, the tree that starts up most forests, as it still does today.

Many traditions speak of this Sacred Tree of all Life being an Apple Tree.

Some Indo Asian, Middle East and European mythology stories speak of this Sacred Apple Tree spouting fresh spring water from around the base of it's trunk.

Fae or Fairy Trees of Ash, Hawthorn, or Rowan are beside most Holy Wells of Ireland, Scotland, Wales and England today, but Apple trees are rarely by these wells now.

Fae trees by Sacred Wells are also known as 'Wishing Trees' where wishes of desire are left through some form of gift, often made of metal.

Some people throw metal coins into wells

Some people bang coins into the Fairy Tree trunks, Ouch! Ouch!, Ouch!

I do not believe either of these metal practices are a good idea, and I do not support them

Fae Trees by wells are also places you can bless and hang wishes of healing through a woven prayer.

Most popular for this are Brighid's Crosses woven from rushes.

Accept The Apple

Prayers and wishes can also be carried through hanging Apples from a tree so maybe it is ok to insert a metal coin into hanging Apple fruits?

To me that idea seems strange ... but we do this with Christmas trees at Yule because we hang baubles, and we hang chocolate coins.

We also place fairies, angels and even goddesses on top of Yule and Christmas trees.

Ancient mythology stories personify the Tree of Life and a goddess handing her Apple to the first man on earth.

It is told that this was the first dowry presented to a man while her serpent of wisdom is entwined within her branches.

Did Adam eat an Apple?

The Garden Of Eden story is a story told by several religions, yet for some reason the story is simplified in the Old Testament in the Bible

Many of us know the story tells of Eden having a Tree of Life that grew 'forbidden fruit', and there is 'the serpent' a simple un-named snake.

What was the 'forbidden fruit' in that story in the Bible's Book of Genesis? It is not mentioned, and 'Apple' is not mentioned at all ???

I suspect the 'Apple' entered into the Adam and Eve story when 16th century Renaissance painters, who created beautiful paintings, added elements of Greek mythology into Biblical scenes.

Apples in sacred tree mythology were popular with ancient Greeks, especially the sacred tree in the Garden of Hera.

The Venus de Milo sculpture of ancient Greece, depicting a naked Venus holding an apple, must have been a huge inspiration for spiritual revelation painters. From ancient Greece until now, many nude portraits in art and sculpture have featured a nude woman holding an Apple.

In both the Greek Garden of Hera story that has since entered the Garden of Eden Story, the Apple is symbolic of coming from a living tree. A Tree Of Life? A tree of Immortality?

In these tales, something corrupted because these stories tell of unconditional love for everything being stopped ... when the Golden Apple is picked. Unconditional love is replaced with desire, temptation, possession and greed.

In several mythologies, Apples are symbolic of love and fertility, and considered as an aphrodisiac, for men. So you may consider that these naked women of art, who are holding Apples, are being seductive in a generous and passionate way.

Various male, sculptors, artists and storytellers compare the shape of Apples to women's breasts.

When the Apple is cut along the core, they also compare what is revealed to a women's vulva. Some say this expression from male artists was amplified after they drank cider, or maybe mead.

Together, religions call all of these artist expressions of desire and temptation = sin !!!

For many of us, those who carry a Catholic guilt, Jewish guilt, Hindu guilt, etc. may spend the rest of our lives working out how to return the Golden Apples to the Tree Of Life.

Do we yearn this so that the immortality of unconditional love returns?

In the Adam and Eve story, a snake tempts Eve to pick an Apple, or forbidden fruit, that is 'ordered' not to be taken by any animal, or any human. So, Eve picks the fruit and shares it with Adam.

Versions of this story tell that separating the Golden Apple from the tree, and eating it for our nutrition, is what caused us to experience and understand grief, sorrow, hunger, and pain.

Isn't this the response for our surrender to curiosity and temptation?

Isn't this what birth into this world is about? Coming into this world as individuals and learning how to become part of the Divine Spirit again?

I believe this act of defiance, the surrender to be born, is what makes us human forever creatures of wonder seeking wisdom and archiving knowledge.

Is this why we, by tradition, give Apples as presents to teachers, as a thank you for them sharing their inspiration of wisdom? Or is an Apple a temptation for the teacher to serve more knowledge?

There is a lot more I am tempted to talk about regarding these symbols.

What do these symbols say to you?

The Tree Of Life,
The Snake,
The Apple,
The Garden of Eden
Adam and Eve.

How did Apples spread around the World?

Where do the Apples we eat come from?

Wild Crab Apples from the edge of forests and light areas within forests have been a staple of many cultures and tribes for 1000s of years. Someone somehow worked out how to graft, culture and create large sweet Apples from at least 12,000 years ago.

It is believed the fruit we call Apple today originated from forest fruit trees in the Middle East. Iran is the current favourite source of the origin of Apples with Iraq and Turkey being close behind.

As Apple trees and its fruit eventually entered into the New World, Apple trees and Apple fruits found home in several cultural mythologies. Celtic, Norse, and Greek mythologies are the best known.

How the English Apple was named is fascinating ...

In Germany, there is the word 'Apfel'.
In Iceland, an Apple is an 'Epli'.
In France, an Apple is a 'Pomme'.

Avalon ...

Celtic mythology includes several stories speaking of places of paradise that existed in different ages that fitted the story told. Whether the story is of Neolithic, Megalithic or Bronze Age times, every one of these ages seem to have islands of orchards.

It should be noted that even the unpalatable harsh and tart wild Crab Apples and Crab Apple trees were revered and the fruits an important staple food through winter. They were used to make mead, jelly, and as a base for medicines.

I am constantly fascinated by the stories of Orchard Island in the middle of Lough Meelagh near Keadue in Co. Roscommon.

The earliest story for there is from one of the many Celtic myth stories telling of cauldrons of plenty, cauldrons that never empty. In these stories the cauldron is stolen, there is a chase, and the cauldron is thrown into a lake.

The theft of Daghda's Cauldron is told in many ways, and one example includes the throwing of his cauldron into a lake.

In this story, the sons of Tuireann stole Daghda's Cauldron. When they were chased, the ever flowing Cauldron got heavier and heavier with its replacing contents slowing them down.

So they threw Daghda's cauldron into Lough Meelagh. Where the cauldron landed in the lake, an island erupted out of the cauldron.

It was on this island that an orchard of Apples grew abundantly, and it became the home of a goddess Lasir

In this Orchard Island story, there was no Tree Of Life but in the centre of the island The Rose Of Sweetness was planted by a bard called Finn, as part of his wooing of Lasir.

This Rose of Sweetness never wilted. It forever provided pollen for the bees to pollinate the Apples, as Rose and Apples are in the same gene family ... also, it is said this is why Apple skins have a rosy red blush :-)

Our local Orchard Island stories are similar to the origin of a well known Apple Orchard Island ...

Accept The Apple

Avalon, the land of Apples, a place of Divine joy, which many relate to Glastonbury Tor, in Somerset, England.

A Welsh word for Apple is 'afal' so it is assumed that's where the word 'Avalon' came from. Also, this is very similar to the German word Apfel.

Mentioning Avalon causes temptation to move on into the legends of Arthur and Merlin. As many other writers go there, I do not need to ...

An Apple A Day, Inspires A Bard To Play ...

Even the Glastonbury Avalon has a story of being formed when a cauldron, gifted to a Bran the Bard, was seized by Barinthus the charioteer who took souls of the dead back to the otherworld.

The cauldron fell off of his chariot and where it fell in the lake to the Otherworld, the Isle Of Avalon formed and an abundant orchard grew there.

Avalon, like our local Orchard Island, in Co. Roscommon, had the presence of a goddess wooed by a Bard. I have never learned of her name.

Here we have Bards in the Apple, or Aval, stories.

Earlier I mentioned about how eating the first Apple symbolizes us becoming human and being filled with all of the human emotions.

A Bard is said to serve Three Strains through music and words that perform for our emotions.

He performs Strains of Sorrow, Joy and Sleep with Sleep being the Dreaming.

Accept The Apple

Avalon is very much symbolic of
The Dreaming.

There is a mythology story that tells of the inside of an Apple being the conduit between our world and the otherworld where our dreams travel through and are responded to.

It is told that within Apple fruits the Sidhe horses, capaill sióga, travel between the two worlds This is why eating Apples is said to inspire us with revelations that we manifest throughout our awakening days.

Many fairy stories tell of demons and evil people. Our imagination, aroused by these stories, reveals the dark side of our dreams.

So, do we accept them as fears
or do we surrender to them?

If we surrender to accept peace,
it is said our dark veils lift within our dreams
to reveal light that will guide us.

To me, this is what Avalon is about. It is a place that the spirit within Apples takes us to.

It is said this spirit from Apples is strongest at Samhain, what many call Halloween today.

For protection through Samhain, now Halloween, there are still places that encourage the tradition of children being sent to bed for the night with an Apple.

They place their Apples under their pillows to protect them from bad dreams and troublesome spirits.

An Apple under a pillow, at any time, is said to enhance protective dreams and loving dreams.

Before I leave this, I love the story of Apple fruits having a trinity of colour

Green said to be a colour of birth,
Yellow for its maturing like the sun across the sky,
Red for the sun as the Apple sinks into
its own sunset at the time of harvesting.

Apple Stories In Ireland ...

I'll give you a few snippets of a couple of stories and they do hold a common theme.

Connla, son of Conn of the Hundred Battles, lived on the Hill of Uisneach. On that hill, he saw a beautiful woman, the goddess Beara, which was invisible to everyone else.

She tempted Connla towards her by throwing an Apple at him. As he caught the Apple, he was surrounded by sea.

The goddess Beara rescued him from the water by pulling him into her glass coracle.

They sailed away together to the 'Plain Of Delight', a place that no other living humans could find. Connla was never seen again

Another version of this story describes Beara as a White Goddess, and sometimes the story calls her Aine, or Grainne.

She is a White Hag posing as a beautiful woman who threw Connla an Apple, and then she vanished. Each day Connla bit into the Apple and each day this increased his longing for her to return and take him to her paradise ...
'Plain Of Delight'.

After 30 days, the beautiful White Goddess returned. Together they sailed west in her glass boat from Uisneach
... and Connla was never seen again

There are stories of Apples ensuring safe passage to Tir na nOg.

A well known story told today is of Oisin riding towards Tir na nOg on a white Sidhe horse that was chasing the White Goddess on a black horse.

The White Goddess was holding an Apple Of Temptation and Immortality.
This apple, and lust for the White Goddess, lured Oisin into Tir na nOg.

Accept The Apple

The ebb and flow of sea and water merges well with Apple symbolism for telling stories about travelling between the two worlds.

Carrying of an Apple symbolizes protection. That is why Apple trees were the trees beside sacred wells. It is very rare to see them by wells now.

By now you may wonder why this Apple feature is a big feature in this book?

Many fairy stories, and other stories, feature forests and woodlands as dark and evil places to visit. Several people may not be entertained by this book encouraging us to go and Bathe In The Fae's Breath in the woods.

Accompanied by an Apple all kinds of wonderful things can happen to us within a forest. I have discovered that offering Apples for people to hold in the woods truly calms their fears, and even helps them to be more inspired.

I thought you might enjoy some of this mythical background to the Apple. Apples were an essential staple food in Ireland before potatoes arrived here. Alas, most crabapple trees are now gone from the forests of Ireland.

Bless the Apple Trees ...

I cannot get through introducing Apple mythology without talking about Wassailing.

This is still a strong tradition of South Wales, Western England, and Wexford in S.E. Ireland.

First step is to be careful with harvesting, though that's a tough one with modern tree shakers.

Traditionally, three Apples should be left on each tree for the Fae, for the fairies. It is said they will bless us well by managing good pollination for a good crop of Apples for the next year.

Another rule is that as Apples are eaten from the personal store, through the winter, always keep enough left over to make an Apple pie for the sheep shearers next May.

So onto Wassailing ...

The ancient tradition of Wassailing Apple trees is intended to awaken the sleeping tree-spirit, protect local people from misfortune, and ensure a good Apple harvest the following year.

Wassailing usually takes place around Yule and involves the farming folk choosing one tree in the orchard to represent all of them.

They chose the oldest tree in the orchard that is called "The Apple Tree Man" tree, because they believe this is where the spirit of the Apple Tree Man lives.

So here is the Wassailing Ritual, very easy really ...

The people present would drink cider after reciting a toast of good health to the tree ... then throw cider over its roots

Next, pieces of bread or toast are soaked in cider and then pushed into where the branches fork into the trunk as far as can be reached

Finally, the Apple trees are danced around

During those three steps with cider, toast and dancing, a song is sung.

After this Wassailing ritual, the Wassailers go to the farmhouse to feed on apple pie, apple flapjacks, and other apple treats.

This is obviously followed with a lot of jollity through stories, songs, dances and thoughts and prayers shared about those not present.

Traditionalists say that Wassailing should never happen where past history of Wassailing is not known. I believe that all Apple trees have a right to be wassailed wherever they grow.

With a growing affinity between trees and humans, today, there is more acceptance to allow in the tradition of Wassailing in its meaningful ways. This tradition is spreading to new places.

Accept The Apple

The Wassailing Song ...

There are several Wassailing Songs
and really each village has its own version.
There is one verse for the cider, one for the toast,
and one for the dancing ....

Here's some new cider we give to thee
To thank you again our dear old apple tree,
May your buds blossom well
So more apples can dwell.
Hats full! Caps full!
Pockets full, and Aprons full!

Here's fresh bread that we baked today
To hold in your bows and not take away.
Now we can drink to thee,
Wish you good health dear tree.
Every bough, Every twig
Bless you now for Apples big.

Here we come a wassailing
Among the leaves so green,
Here we come a wandering
Where all of us are seen.
Bringing love to share with you
And bless with wassail too,
Protect us all from ill and pain
So next year we meet here again

Why Do Trees Whisper? :

This is from an Estonian legend. I will explain why I have included it in this book later.

This story starts in the early days of humans on earth. The trees had been on this earth for millions of years before us humankind were born here.

A disruption in Paradise had happened, which is a story well told, and there was no longer enough food and shelter provided for humans. All humans were forced out of Paradise and had to toil hard for their food and shelter.

One of these men went into the forest to cut wood to build a home, clear land to grow food and create a store of firewood. He had already learned to create an axe and other tools.

The first tree he came to was a Pine tree. But as soon as the man lifted his axe he heard a voice from the tree cry out.

Why Do Trees Whisper?

"Please don't strike me!
Can't you see my sticky tears that are already coming out of my trunk?
If you strike me with your axe,
it will bring you bad luck!"

The man looked at the sticky sap weeping from the tree trunk, so he moved on further into the forest. He stopped at a Spruce tree and raised his axe, and the Spruce tree shouted at him!

"Don't cut me down.
You will find my wood has little use for you
as my wood is twisted and knotty."

After a big frustrating sigh, the man went on through the forest until he came to an Alder tree.

Once more he raised his axe to strike
but the tree shrieked at him!

"Be careful, do not strike me with your axe.
When I am cut, blood runs from my heart.
It will stain my wood, your axe will turn red,
my blood will seep through your clothes
and will never wash out."

The man looked up at the sky and yelled!!!

"How am I to get wood to build a shelter, make fire, and clear ground for food? Every tree here cries out and pleads to not be cut down."

The man left the forest and talked to the priest of the new community outside of the forest. He asked the priest what he could do.

The priest went into the forest for awhile,
then returned and said to the man
"Return to the forest now
and no tree will talk back at you."

The man returned to the forest, lifted his axe, chopped down one tree, then another tree, and another.

He kept on chopping until he had built a shelter, cleared land to farm, and had fuel for heat.

Through doing all of that, not one tree protested! But, the trees were not happy !!!

They dared not complain and be visited by that priest again. Why, I do not know. What power did the priest have over them?

The trees now whisper softly,
each time humans enter the forest.

Why Do Trees Whisper?

When you approach trees in a wood or forest anywhere, have you noticed that we can hear them softly whispering to each other?

This is the sound of trees gently complaining about their poor treatment that woods and forests receive in the hands of humans.

How can we be kind to them?

I got most of that story from a book with a long title ... "Hidden Stories in Plants: Unusual and Easy-to-Tell Stories from Around the World Together with Creative Things to Do While Telling Them" by Anne Pellowski. It seems to be unpublished now, and only in secondhand bookstores.

This is a simple story that reminds us of difficult decisions we are positioned to make when we cut down trees.

Add to that, the decision to clear an area of Nature that has been there for 1000s of years.

We do this because we need shelter, food, and heat. We are no longer a hunter-gatherer race, so this is what we know.

These days we pay others to clear away Nature for our needs, or at least pay someone to give us permission to clear away a chunk of Nature ... someone like the priest in this story maybe?

As a child, I was fortunate to have a woodland glen beside where I lived as a den. One day, developers turned up and took most of those woods away to build houses for people.

As a child, this hurt me and made me angry. I wondered what the trees and animals who lived there thought of this?

The ever essential Tree Huggers ...

When some people see a forest, or consider growing a forest, they may only think about how they can profit from it. Crop forestry rarely receives consideration for the rights to life that a forest and its inhabitants have.

I think one of the greatest flaws of humans is our lack of respect for any life that is not human, especially tree and plant life that has no obvious brain mechanism.

One way we can respect all life, I believe, is build a relationship with living things that are not human.

Storytellers through the ages have done this by personifying animals, plants and trees. Even today, post a picture, on Facebook, of a tree with a half door on the trunk with a mouse in a hat and pinafore looking out, and we sigh "ahhh!'. If it was just a tree, or even a naked regular wild mouse on a tree, we might not notice.

So, how about the idea of treating the tree with the same courtesy as we may have when we approach someone we don't know yet?

We would not lean upon the stranger would we? We would not pull his or her hair, or even bang 'wishing' coins into the stranger's body?

Once you've made friends with a tree, continue to care and treat the tree just as you do with human friends. Hugs, of course, strengthen bonds with trees, but applying all of our senses can do much more.

A fun thing to do is put an ear up against a tree trunk to hear tree echoes within on a windy or breezy day. Different sounds come from different tree species. Also, different wood densities within trunks vibrate different sounds. Broadleaved trees sound very different through the seasons.

Select a tree and listen during
Spring, Summer, Fall and Winter.
Each season serves different sounds.

Get close to a tree activates our smell sense too. Taste comes from the components we breathe too, but also from the tastes of flowers, blossoms, fruits, and seeds, through the changing seasons. Of course, be well aware of what is nourishing and what is toxic. For example, you would sustain very respectful contact with a Yew tree.

So, our relationship with a tree bonds through touch, sound, smell, taste, and we must not forget sight. Stop for a moment and watch what is happening around a tree.

Watch how rain water flows down a trunk and see what happens. Watch what happens to the look and mood of a tree through different lights such as sunshine, cloud, dawn, dusk, and moon at night.

Observe a single favourite tree through all of these changes, if you can.

By getting to know a tree, and the other trees, plants and wildlife around it, a long term friendship can develop with a tree.

Through engaging in this seemingly hippie tree hugging relationship we develop a very different value for nature and how we integrate. Actually, we do not integrate with nature, but are reminded how we are part of it.

We cannot deny it. Nature is not currency for acquisition and ownership but for sharing.

Mother Trees ...

Several people have talked to me about the work of forester Suzanne Simard from the University of British Columbia, Canada.

Google 'Suzanne Simard mother trees' and you will get several links to video clips, TEDtalks, and articles on her work and vision of 'Mother Trees' and forest integration.

Suzanne's work seems to have commenced when she discovered that the vast underground tree root systems are like giant brains when they integrate with the spawn webs of fungi.

She discovered that the exchange network of tree roots and fungi spawn threads work like neurons in our brains that constantly exchange 'messages'.

When we walk into a forest, it's likely that all the trees, all of the species together, are networked with each other in some way, as far as we can see.

Suzanne claims that trees are also transmitting resources through this network to help out other trees as well as the plants and fungi in between them.

Capping all of her research are what she calls "mother trees". These are the elder trees within a forest that are several hundred years old. When they are about to die, Suzanne claims they start passing their resources off to the next generation of mature trees around them.

She describes this as being like passing a wand from one generation to the next. So is that what our human family trees are all about?

By forming relationships with trees and forests, I passionately believe that we can understand forests and regain our forest culture again. The 'law' of animals is usually to kill what will be eaten. These are natural sustaining 'laws' that I believe we should apply similarly to our trees and forests.

Instead of our linear attitude of growing controlled crops, followed by clear-felling, I believe we should encourage the creation of forests as singular living breathing organs.

As humans, we depend on forests for materials for food, medicine, crafts, construction and fuel. I believe we can still respect the forest through selective thinning and replanting along with the effects of wildlife distribution of seeds, bugs, fungi and compost.

Also we should consider coppicing more. It is very sustainable as we only harvest the tree tops without harming the 'brain' of the roots.

Clear-fell loggers find it easier and more profitable than thinning management. This is forestry controlled by spreadsheets. Our economy, today, is controlled by spreadsheets. I believe the consequences of spreadsheet economics causes many people to feel disconnected, longing and unaware of the effects of what we consume.

Replace spreadsheet bred policies with community human involvement and we would experience a very different and more wholesome culture that would evolve among us.

Clear-felling clears away 'Mother Trees' who will not be able to pass along messages or pass along the resources to the next generation of trees. When loggers take away 'Mother Trees', they wipe out forest communities.

Think of other areas of human activity where spreadsheet economics, politics, and even religion, is driving this.

Yes, all of this is a reminder of the Avatar movie, isn't it?

Who's Woods Are These? :

Who's woods are these,
Who rides by to seize
These woods where I once played
I am told I am trespassing today.

That birch I once climbed to swing down low,
That elder I cut to carve a flute,
With rowan I strung a bow.
Breathing sensual aromas,
Touching a bubbling stream,
Where I would sit for hours to incubate a dream.

But someone fenced my woods today;
An agent of those who moralize
the freedom to betray,
And show me their nailed growling warning sign;
To keep me out,
Keep you out,
Keep your children out .... and crying.

And the man with the axe said,
We have only claimed ...

Bathing In The Fae's Breath

Where nobody came any more.
What ??? ...you may exclaim!
Let that man with the axe never speak no more.
Lets be with the trees hugging, breathing,
Pulsating life to explore.

So who's woods are these?
Into every public forest in Ireland please,
Occupying the woods so nobody else will dare
To seize them, because the forests are for our care,

For as long as we are there, sharing, airing, caring

The Handsome Frog

The Handsome Frog :

Most of us are familiar with a Brother's Grimm fairy story "The Frog Prince"?

If not, here's a snappy super short version ...

Princess goes to play in the woods,
takes a golden ball to play with there,
her favourite toy,
drops it into pond,
a frog appears
and offers to rescue the ball for her,
in return for being able to visit her at the castle.
Princess believes the castle is too far away
for the frog to visit,
so agrees with the terms and gets her ball back.
Frog gets the ball
... and does, indeed, hop over to visit the castle
and the King orders his princess daughter
to honour her agreement.
She shares her food plate with the frog,
very reluctantly,

then frog goes to sleep with her in bed,
cuddled up close.
This is repeated
over three evenings and three nights,
then on the following morning,
after the third night,
the frog has become a handsome prince,
with beautiful blue eyes,
who spins a yarn about being under a spell
from a wicked witch,
so they get married,
indulge in royal abundance,
indulgence and gluttony,
and live happily ever after ....ahhh :-)

... and millions of women have been seeking for a Prince, just like that for themselves, ever since they heard that story ... or have they?

Many of us have heard that tale in several ways, haven't we? Here's a potted history of it ...

Within the first publication of the Grimms Tale, 1812 I believe, when the morning after the third night arrived, the Princess was angry with this 'carry-on' and threw the frog against the wall.
Out of the 'splat' on the wall
the handsome Prince appeared!

The Handsome Frog

By 1823, there had been accumulated concerns about exposing children to such gross violence from a 'fairy story', so the story altered and toned down. Now, the Princess woke up after the third night to find a Prince already sleeping next to her, no splatting required.

The origin of this Frog Prince story goes back into earlier oral tradition. The Grimms story appears to have come from a Scottish Gaelic tale that was translated into English as 'The Well Of The World's End'. This was first published during 1549 and printed on an early Caxton printing machine, This pre-dates Shakespeare.

I will come back to the content of this Scottish story later.

The English translation of this Scottish story is what the Brother's Grimm wrote their 'The Frog Prince' from, and they also pulled 'Cinderella' from this same old Scottish story too.

The Brothers Grimm toned down the violence a bit because in the Scottish story the Princess slices off the frog's head, but out of the frog's torso leaps a handsome blue eyed Prince.

By 1857, there were more accumulated concerns. This time it was about the Princess waking up to discover she had been sleeping with a male handsome Prince beside her while still unmarried.

It was uncertain that her bed sharer was still a frog when she went to sleep.

The story was still regarded as immoral and even pornographic. So the sleeping in the bed part was taken out of the story. The frog did return back into her bed, though, in the 1905 published version.

So how did the 'kissing the frog', that turns into a Prince, arrive in this story? Surely, kissing a frog is a much less violent way of telling this story than chopping his head off?

Nobody seems to know when kissing replaced violence in the 'Frog Prince' story. It is suspected to have happened through translations and re-tellings between 1823 and 1857. During that time, the 'kiss' took on its own mythology.

It is said that the first introduction of 'kissing' in this story involved much more than an innocent kiss on the cheek or forehead.

The Handsome Frog

The urban legend is that this 'kissing' version of the Grimms story became popular in 19th-century pornography and prostitution role playing.

This sensual re-telling may have also influenced the idea of cutting out the bed scenes from the Grimms story after 1857. By order of Queen Victoria maybe, as this change was shortly after her becoming queen.

I have rambled long enough to serve a background to this Frog Prince story before explaining why I have included it here in this 'Bathing In The Fae's Breath' book.

At this point, I think its a good idea for me to step back again into the older Scottish story, that the Grimms brothers wrote their version from.

This is 'The Well At The World's End' story.

In this older Scottish story, instead of a 'King' we have a 'Chieftain' featured.
So, he is not the top dog of the nation.

His daughter was not a 'Princess'
but, simply, was 'his daughter'.

The Chieftain had lost his wife, his daughter's mother, to a plague. Even so, being a local chieftain, who had lost a wife, caused him to be a 'good catch' for other women. He would still have the wealth of lands and services of people to work these lands.

So, the Chieftain married another woman. Alas, as was common then, his new wife was not in love with him. She was in love with sharing his life of position and wealth.

In this old story, the new wife brings along her two daughters from a previous marriage. Her former husband was killed in battle???

So what we have in this older story is a cruel stepmother situation brewing with the Chieftain's real daughter getting rough treatment when the Chieftain was away, which he often was.

Oh, how I can personally relate to this because I had a father who had lost his wife, was quite well off, but mainly worked overseas. He married again to a woman who was really after his 'position' and financial security to help fund her and expensive indulgences of her two wayward sons. I can feel for that Chieftain's daughter in this story.

The Handsome Frog

In this Scottish story, the cruel 'stepmother' orders the Chieftain's daughter to collect water in a sieve. She tells her that until she does this she will never have a husband, good health, or wealth in her life.

As the Chieftain's daughter tried to get water from a well into the sieve, a frog appeared and offered to show her a way to do this. His request was to visit her at her 'Chieftain' father's house.

This was agreed, so the frog showed her how to weave in clay and grasses into the sieve's holes and bake it in the sun so that the sieve became a pot to carry water in.

The stepmother and stepsisters were, of course, horrified when the Chieftain's daughter appeared back home with a sieve full of water.

Their horrors soon turned to laughter, though, when the frog did call at their house to be with the Chieftain's daughter. The stepmother ordered the Chieftain's daughter to keep her promise and share her food and bed with this frog.

As I mentioned earlier, this is the early version of this story that includes the head chopping scene after the third night.

The Chieftain's daughter could not take any more abusive frog fun entertaining her stepmother and daughters ... so it was 'away with the frog'.

But, when the handsome prince emerged from the frog torso, they got married.

The Prince became the Gaelic King, and she became Queen ruling over all of the Chieftains, including their wives and their daughters.

Obviously, this was not now a funny situation for her stepmother and stepsisters now.

So there we have a section of this Scottish origin story that the Grimms brothers separated into their 'Cinderella' story.

What interests me today are some of the modern interpretations of this wild rural Scottish story that eventually became a Grimms Story..

**The 'feminine activists'
are right onto this one !!!**

Our modern moralities and political correctness do indeed cause us to question this story now.

Think about this story for awhile ....

The Handsome Frog

In the Grimms story, the frog prince appears to be described as being an innocent young man who encounters two kinds of female characters.

On one side, there is the 'evil witch' woman who turned him into a frog.

On the other side, the "gullible princess" woman who sacrifices herself to violence, or to 'kissing', a frog so that he turns into the Prince.

Another character in the Grimms story is the Patriarchal King father. He expects his daughter to be "a good girl" and fulfill her promise to the frog, even though the frog had manipulated her into making the promises. How fair is that?

For a start, is this story teaching girls that they are either "evil" or "gullible"?

Is this teaching boys to become manipulating Princes through using pathetic "I've been emotionally and physically wounded by another woman" pick up line stories?

Now for my alternatives ways
of telling this story :-)

Let's get back on the topic of
'Bathing In The Fae's Breath' here.

What if the witch in the story ...
wasn't really evil at all?

What if the handsome blue-eyed Prince ...
was not as innocent as he later claimed to be?

I find myself asking, "what if the Prince was a real nuisance to a country woman through objecting against her foraging for herbs and foods in his father's forest?

Maybe this Prince thought he could get away with some lusty kissing with this 'peasant' woman in the woods ... only have some herbs rammed down him that turned him into a frog, or at least into something visually 'ugly'.

At the other side of the forest, we have an innocent, gullible Princess playing in the forest. She drops her golden ball into the water, and the Prince sees this as 'opportunity'.

So he manipulates her into having a good mooch of food, comfort, and maybe good kissing at her father's castle.

The Handsome Frog

In a feminist expression and re-translation of this story, the Princess did exactly the opposite of what girls and women have been taught by the Grimms version for many years.

In the 'feminist' version, the Princess certainly did not kiss the frog. She also did not listen to her father's expectation to fulfill a promise from someone that had taken advantage of her. Also, she was was not a "nice girl" through the traditional definition of "nice girl."

Their conclusion to this story mentions nothing about the Princess marrying a handsome Prince and living 'happily' ever after, but of a Princess claiming her power and owning her voice.

This is what the 'evil witch' of the forest had already learned and personally caused the Frog Prince's to have his frog spell predicament in the first place.

Up until recently, and it still happens, when girls and women claim their own 'voice' ... they are called "mean," "cruel," "bitches," and even "witches".

Now, to get into my 'alternative' version of the 'Frog Prince' story ...

I call this the 'Handsome Frog' ...

As I mentioned, we may question who is this 'evil witch' in the traditional story? In my story, she is not 'evil' at all but a wise woman of the forest and Nature, who lives her entire life around this relationship.

Now what about the Prince? In defense of frogs, why do we have to assume a frog is 'ugly'?

In the Grimms 'fairy story', the frog is 'ugly' unless he morphs into a handsome blue eyed Prince. A 'handsome prince' is also a man who inherits a load of money, uses it to keep the Princess eternally happy with physical comforts, while he affords going off to play with his mistresses.

To me, this Grimms story, or the older Scottish story, is not about the circumstances of two women, the 'evil witch' and the 'gullible Princess' ... but about two different environments and cultures.

On one side, we have the Princess from the Castle, and on the other side we have the Frog in the Forest. Castle and Forest, hmmm, what thoughts does this set-off?

Has anyone seen the Secret Of Kells beautiful animated movie, which tells this comparison and proverb very well?

I ask, how can this be a 'fairy story' when the happy ending is about a life of probable selfish human indulgence. I feel this is totally against the Fae! It's more like a Fairy Nightmare. To me, I think this should be a story that teaches us that frogs are 'cool', smart, and even 'handsome'.

We should be attracted to frogs, be encouraged to learn about them and where they live, and not expect them to become something else.

I can understand the strong Patriarchal leanings in the Grimms story. This was the protected preserved culture of their time. The worst effect of this story, though, seems to be the intent of influencing people to be fearful of the forest. It is a source of fear of entering forests that people still have today.

Within Grimm's tales, forests are described as being dangerous places of 'evil witches' and 'ugly slimy frogs'. In other Grimms stories the forests are places where we starve, get poisoned and get eaten up, and are never seen of and heard of again.

In these Grimms style stories, we are also told that Castles and the lifestyles lived within them are all 'happily ever after'. Happiness is from gluttony of food, fine furniture, fine sheets and bedding, and servants to serve our whims without question.

Within Castles and their farming communities are we being told to consume and honour the human pecking order from slave or servant up the pyramid to the chieftain and king? Are we told that the Chieftains and Kings at the top of the pecking order are also closest to the Divine?

Through an indulgent consuming culture, are we also being lured to avoid connection to the forest?

Are we influenced to consume our forests, and other things, to create all of this human created 'finery' within our 'Castle' realms?

Is beauty, from human creations, from within the 'Castle' culture far superior to anything that Nature can supply us with?

I believe that through this false superiority we are being taught that Nature is ugly. Is it only there to serve human consumption that creates those 'happily ever after' dreams?

I can imagine another story ...

With this I imagine two castles,
one on each side of a huge forest.

Once upon a time, A a young boy Prince, started wondering what was in the forest, beside the castle, that he was brought up in.

He went into the forest and met a young woman who lives there and was raised to live with what's in the forest. She lived as part of all that lives, breathes, competes and share's in the forest. He fell in love with her, believing love would be forever while living with her in the forest.

There, he learned the ways of the forest ...

Over time, the fine 'castle' clothes that he entered into the forest with faded and tore up. He replaced these clothes with clothes more adaptable to what is needed to live in the forest. Maybe his clothes were woven from leather, hairs and plants gathered from the woods.

Then, entering the forest from the other side, along comes a Princess curious about what goes on there, and she has her golden ball with her ???

With this version of the story, maybe it was not a slimy frog that manipulated the Princess in the forest, but a former Prince lad in slimy woodland clothes.

Did the Princess remind him
of his own former indulgent Prince's life?
Did this encounter with her tempt him to
return to have another go at indulgent royal life?

So, the former prince visits the Princess at the castle she lives in.

After a good feed, he actually has a bath where he took off all of his slimy clothes ... and nakedly revealed himself to the Princess as a handsome blue eyed Prince.

What happens after that is your own story to create ...

Exercise your visions ...

What I invite you to do here is
re-think this story,
carry it with you,
ask questions about what it is saying to you
but do not expect answers.

Do this with all fairy stories!

With this story, visualize all you can about the Castle, how and why it is there and how the King or Chieftain created their riches and wealth.

What was destroyed, consumed and sacrificed to enable them to have the indulgent lives they have in this story?

How many people surrender their lives to serve the pampered lives of these royal family people in the castle?

Next, visualize the Forest as a happy place where the trees found their own homes there through the unseen 'gardening' of the Divine.

Vidualize a forest not created by humans to serve an illusion of manicured beauty,

Visualize the forest as being a place where waters from springs are free to spout, heal and roam. A forest where plants are there to nourish and heal us when we need them, growing in a place that is not a 'kingdom', but a space ruled by something unseen and unconditional.

Through visualizing these two different realms of Castle and Forest, could you believe a 'fairy story' is where the witches are kind, frogs are handsome? To me, that's an honest Fairy Story.

Let's change the story to tell of a 'kind' Witch but maybe an 'evil' King, though setting up sides is not very wholesome really.

But, if the King wants to expand his castle, and his farm lands around the castle, to indulge more ... he would have to take some of the Forest away.
Is this 'happily ever after' thinking?

Here's a wish that you will become blessed if you believe in 'fairy stories' that tell us about Nature's wealth and health that is being cared for.

If Nature is told of as being a place to return to be happy, be loved, be provided for, and not a place to bring golden balls to, though do bring an apple ...
I believe you will become 'Happily Ever After'.

Song Of Airmid :

When thinking of Irish and Celtic healing deities, especially Goddesses, most minds think of Brighid, or maybe Anu and Aine. The stories of Airmid are few, but what a remarkable image of healing and well-being she serves and teaches us.

Airmid, also known as Airmed or Airmeith, was a member of the Tuatha De Danaan. It is among stories about them that she appears.

Deeds of the Tuatha De Dannan ...

The Tuatha De Dannan are discussed a lot on social media. They were an ancient race that arrived on the shores of what is now Ireland. Despite many debates, nobody is sure where they came from or when they arrived on these shores.

Their race was full of colourful characters. Bards have told many fairy stories about the deeds of these mysterious people who are told of as having beyond earthly magical powers.

Airmid is told of as being the daughter of Diancecht, the Father of Medicine for the Tuatha De Danaan. She also had four brothers. Miach, being one of them and the other three come up as different names in different stories.

Airmid also had a sister, Etan, a poet inspired by the work and skills of Airmid and Etan was wife of Ogma, who I will speak of soon.

Diancecht and his children were the 'only' family of Medicine, Healing, Wellness and Magic for the De Dannan. He was very possessive of their position. He believed his family held the exclusive right to the profession of healing others.

The Tuatha De Dannan story, on Erin, seems to begin when they fought against earlier arrivals, the Firbolgs. In that battle the Firbolg King, Eocchid MacEric, was slain but not before Nuada, the King Of The Tuatha De Dannan, had his arm severed off in battle.

Diancecht, and his son and daughter, Miach and Airmid, were immediately called upon to attend to Nuada to attempt to save his arm and save his life. Alas, Diancecht did not have the skills to sew back Nuada's arm to his shoulder, so he attached a silver arm instead.

The De Dannan constitution of that time forbade any man with wounds, blemishments or bodily imperfections to rule as King. So Nuada was retired to an abundant farmland that is still named after him today, Magh Nuada, Maynooth.

However, together, Miach and Airmid knew how to preserve Nuada's arm. Diancecht's skills were limited to understanding bones and the alchemy of metals extracted from rocks.

Miach understood the healing of flesh and nerves, and Airmid was fast learning about plants and how to prepare and use them for healing.

The Rage of Diancecht ...

The replacement king Brés caused another huge battle, this time against the Fomorians.

Without Diancecht knowing, Miach and Airmid travelled to Nuada and successfully connected his real arm back onto to his shoulder.

By being unblemished again,
Nuada could lead as King again.

During the first day of this second battle of Moytura, at Samhain, that many people call Halloween today, Diancecht, Miach and Airmid attended to the wounded by the Well Of Slaine. This was a rich water spring that overflowed into what is now named Lough Arrow.

When a wounded warrior was brought to the Well Of Slaine, his body was immediately immersed in its water. Not only did this bring him back to life, but also made him well enough to return to the battle the next day. During this first day of battle, their healing work was very successful.

During this day, Diancecht's inner anger was festering. He was jealous of the healing work done by his son and daughter as it was more skilled than anything he had learned to do. He was also concerned that they may teach their skills outside of the family and no longer be exclusive to them.

The second day of this Samhain battle was a dark day. Diancecht's rage and jealousy caused him to kill his son Miach during the night after the first day of battle. The killing was not easy. Each time Diancecht's drew his sword to maim his son, Miach healed himself instantly and carried on fighting his father.

Diancecht's anger finally caused him to cut off Miach's head, and he immediately pulled out his brain from his fallen skull and destroyed it ... before Miach had a chance to revive himself again.

Diancecht then took Miach's body far away from the Well Of Slaine so nobody had a chance to attempt to heal him.

Airmid rising early, saw they had gone and saw the blood, so she went to seek after them. This left the Well Of Slaine unattended.

The Fomorians filled it up with stone and created a huge stone mound over where the well was; that also blocked the water's flow into the Lough.

The Tuatha De Dannan could no longer access the well and its waters for healing again

Add to this, Nuada, despite full recovery, was completely slain during that second day of this battle, along with about two-thirds of the De Dannan warriors.

After this second day's battle, it looked like the Fomorians were about to be the new complete rulers of Erin. There was a twist of good fate on the third day, but that's another story ...

Airmid's Cloak ...

Airmid caught up with her father burying her brother Miach's body. Diancecht ignored her being there and walked away saying, "I do not have any sons, I do not have any daughters".

Where Miach was buried does not seem to have been speculated by storytellers. Wherever it was, Airmed stayed there day and night through the following winter.

When Spring returned, she awoke to see the entire grave area over Miach's body covered in flowers and plants in the shape of Miach's body.

The story tells us that 365 plants were there and that each of them was growing on the part of the body they could nourish and heal.

Yes, I know it's hard to imagine 365 plants growing in just the area of a human torso, but that's what the story reveals.

365 is a symbolic number, and perhaps a simple message teaching us that Airmid's herbs, if foraged carefully and stored well, can be medicine and nourishment for any time throughout the year.

It is as if Airmid was already teaching us that we can have fresh herbs in spring or stored dried herbs through winter.

To me, 365 also verifies that her craft works through nature's cycles, and not through a systematic linear of disease-medicine-cure.

To continue this story, Airmid spread out her apron that stretched into a large blanket. She placed each of the 365 herbs there to dry, in the same order they appeared within the shape of Miach.

Her wish was to show this plant medicine wisdom to anyone who wanted to learn.

News of Airmid's discovery reached Diancecht. Again, in a rage, he returned to Airmid, pulled her blanket of herbs and shook it.

The plants on the blanket scattered, and he scolded and reminded Airmid that healing was the work of their family and for nobody else to learn.

Diancecht demanded Airmid to return with him to help dismantle the Heapstown Cairn, as it is now called, to try and reclaim their healing well again.

It was through doing this unending work of trying to remove the big mound of stones placed there by 1000s of Fomorian warrior that Diancecht and Airmid ended their days on earth.

Today, bards and storytellers speak of Airmid being the 'Queen' of the Fae in the forests'.

Maybe Airmid is still Present as the unseen conductor of the Fae, ensuring that plants are where humans and all animals need to forage.

Her whispers arouse our instincts to recognize what plants we need for well being and healing when we need them, if we would just listen.

Was I listening when during my stroke I rushed outside to gather Hawthorn?

Airmid of the Fae ...

Stories tell of birds and animals, especially hares, being couriers of Airmid's plants and helping to distribute the seeds to where they need to be.

As the forests decline in Erin and around the world, it is easy to wonder if the spirit of Diancecht is forever turning Airmid's cloak away to stop her spreading the family's healing ways.

Even though I mentioned that a squirrel can no longer jump tree to tree from Dublin to Sligo, a hare can certainly get across a farmer's field to the next woodland to maybe share some seeds.

Stories tell of Airmid's Cloak still being incomplete. She still needs the senses and wisdom of people, with love of life, to continue to forage for the missing herbs to complete the Cloak of Airmid. It is 'her' mission to bring well-being and Presence of love and life back to all people.

The story of Aimid is another of those precious stories of loss and renewal. To me, it is another story that explains to us the unseen changes of life between Autumn, through Winter and into Spring. Airmid's story teaches us to prepare to enter her sacred spaces, the Native Forest.

When we do, shed our skin of concerns, guilt, sorrow and fear. Be free with our quiet questions that may ask for help for ourselves, our family or community.

I suggest, carry an apple with ashes from your fire. Clean it with water within Airmid's forest 'temple'. Use the apple as an image of you peeling off your baggage and leaving it behind.

Welcome the presence of Airmid. You do not need to speak her name, just accept she is with you.

Forgive the stories of Diancecht as they are probably hearsay. To me, stories about him seem to be like stories spread by those in pain needing to tell stories to provide a blame.

I read this whole story differently. I read and think of Diancecht as being of the stone of the earth, Miach as being of the soil and Airmid being of all that grows from the soil.

After Lughnasadh, like the bird and like the hare, we bring seeds to the forest, and may take seeds to plant elsewhere else. Unlike the squirrel, we can still get from Dublin to Sligo.

Song Of Airmid

An Airmid song I once heard ...

She changes everything she touches
and everything she touches changes.
She changes everything she touches
and everything she touches changes .
Everything lost is found again,
in a new form, in a new way.
Everything hurt is healed again,
in a new life, in a new day.

The earth is alive, so we are alive.
Its soil is alive, so we can be alive,
With courage, we are healed,
as Airmid bathes us.
With courage, we are healers,
when we bathe others with her breath.

Airmid is a story. I feel, she not a deity to worship or we will miss the teaching. She is a story of the 'unseen' that has been given a name and a story to arouse us. Perhaps her story inspires us to follow what it shows us, what it teaches us.

So please go forth and always search, to complete the 'Cloak of Airmid'.

Ask others that wander around the plants and trees to sense them and forage from them.

Ask what these people know about trees and plants and can share with you. Share what you know to bless their wisdom too.

As her story teaches, all of this fellowship sharing helps Airmid to complete her cloak again.

Airmid's story seems like the backbone of the biodiversity permaculture movement as many medicinal plant species are still found only in the wild and cannot be successfully cultivated.

When you are not in a forest and are privileged to have space in your yard for a garden, it is wonderful if you can devote an area outside to be a special shrine or altar to remember Airmid by.

This may be a place where you can feel comfortable to ask her blessings for the growth and preparation of your herbs, and for her to ask you to share what she teaches, in return.

When we stop and stand, or sit, or lay, within a grove of trees, and listen to nearby water ... we can feel the weight of our used worn 'baggage' lift from us. Spiritual and emotional wounds begin to heal.

The healing power of plants goes far beyond physical medical preparations.

When we delight in the colour and scent of blooming flowers, fresh leaves, and the enchanting fragrances of pinenes we know the healing power of Airmid is Present.

In Spring, we become aware of how she creates life from death, bringing healing from the winter grave of Miach, now a living blanket over the cold stone and metals of Diancecht

Through our Bards In The Woods meet ups, we include seeking to help Airmid, and Airmid seeks us to help us ...
when we 'Bathe in the Fae's Breath'.

As I listen to bards and storytellers through my life, and more recently the poems of the Bards In The Woods, it always reveals remarkable 'inspiration'. We must never become separated from the root of Gaelic faith and tradition. No scripted rites are needed for 'inspiration'.

When I join 'scholarly' debates, there is always a strong emphasis on 'citations'. Citations are merely references to more books and journals containing more citations of older books and journals.

Somewhere in the deeper ancestry of all books there is the origin of the 'Prophets of Presence'.

These are the people who scribed something from inspiration, from their Divine experience. Even if calibrated instruments were used, the words scribed are still inspiration.

This is the strength and usefulness of poetry. It is an invocation of what our senses are telling us. Time spent in the forests among the trees, plants, fungi, water and wildlife places us where all poets have been through the centuries.

Even if you are not feeling inspired to write your own poetry, there are 1000s of books available with samples of appropriate poetry to share with others in the forests. Modify any of them for your needs and feelings if you wish too. Airmid responds, and soon you will be inspired to write your own too.

While talking about books, do you know about the 'Carmina Gadelica' collection.

Originally, it was a 6 volume compilation containing poetic material in Scottish Gaelic that has now been made available in English.

This is an incredible rich source of literature that links the wild nature world to poetic verses, charms, and folk-beliefs.

Song Of Airmid

There are prayers, hymns, charms, incantations, blessings, proverbs, lore and stunning tree, plant, wildlife and water lore gathered from the Gaelic-speaking regions of Scotland. These were collected between 1860 and 1909 by exciseman and folklorist Alexander Carmichael.

Near the start of this chapter, I mentioned Airmid's sister Etan, a poet inspired and guided by Airmid's unseen spirit. The story of Etan is that through her poetry she helped people on earth to visualize, memorize and become part of Airmid's realm on earth.

Fae's Breath on my life,
Stone, earth, and its bounty
Inspires me to share

Healing beyond strife,
Due to a sister's love
I am here for you

Etan's poetic memory of trees and plants is said to have inspired her husband Ogma, into creating a language that became easy for people to understand and be taught to the people they met.

Airmid and Etan the little known women behind the successful Ogma of the Ogham.

Introducing Ogma :

Artwork by Milena Rooney
of Spiral Path Designs

This set is inspired by what may have been the creation of the ancient Ogham alphabet.

Introducing Ogma

I am fascinated about how sounds were originally matched to and scribed to symbols. How was this matchmaking decided and shared?

Going back further, how did sounds evolve to be linked together into words, into sentences, paragraphs, and then into complete texts. All of this compiled so that one person could understand the meaning of sounds spoken by another human. Conversation is a remarkable achievement.

Wonder too at the acceleration of this when spoken language became scribed and stored as libraries that other people could read and translate back into silent sound and meaning.

As you will have read through my 'Bathing In The Fae's Breath' text, I have also been a lifelong lover of trees, especially their mythology and the inspiration their Presence inspires..

A local legend, of where I live in Co. Sligo, tells of Ogham being first taught near where I live by an ancient teacher called Ogma. It is said that when he applied specific sounds to a set of 20 symbols his students were asked to memorize the symbols according to the names of native trees and shrubs. This became spoken of in stories as being the 'Memory Of Trees'.

How I discovered this Ogham mythology ...

The first time I learned a version of Ogma's Tale Of The Trees was on the island of Iona. This is a strange place to do so, as Iona is an island with very few trees. There are some native Hawthorn trees and a dozen or less planted beech trees close to what was the parish church.

Maybe this has a connection to Columcille, a Ghael, landing on Iona and meeting the Picts and bringing their traditions together at this place.

When I was first introduced to some meaning about Ogham, I learned Ogma's Tale of The Trees as being a set of 20 symbols associated with trees and shrubs. I was shown a mythology key for each tree and shrub, with each key representing a rite of living and learning.

On Iona, I also learned about a mythology called 'the Four Cilles Of Instruction'.

At the time, I thought it was remarkable how these 'Four Cilles' seems to have some relationship to the Four Treasures of the Tuatha De Dannan.

Introducing Ogma

As I was a keen astrology student and practitioner, I could connect a relationship between the 'Four Cilles' and the Four Quarters of a Chaldean or Babylonian astrology chart. That is a popular charting system with western style astro diviners today.

I also learned that the 'Four Cilles' related to the Four Seasons of a year cycle, but not as divination for the year. The Four Seasons relationship is to the Four Seasons of our life. So, following this is, indeed, just like the divination of the Four Quarters of an astrology chart.

The original 20 symbols of the Ogham are split into Four Scales, that some diviners call an acime, or acimi in plural. In this project, I have decided to call the four scales the Four Seasons.

Each acime, or what I call Season, has Five Symbols, meaning Five Sounds. Each of these sounds relates to a tree or shrub. Five Sounds in sequence is also a Pentatonic Scale. This alone has quite an expanded mythology too.

It is said that in ancient times language, poetry and music were all spoken as the same. Ancients would sing their conversations, or speak their songs. Both were identical.

Origin of my Ogma's Tale Of The Trees stories ...

Over the years, at least 40 of them since learning the Keys of Ogma's Tale Of The Trees on Iona, I have expanded these 20 Keys of the Trees of Ogham into a series of small stories or poems.

For several years, I improvised them when asked. Today, I have become more structured as my story poems are written down, though the written versions have lines changed within them quite often. They are not just story poems any more but include songs, tunes and even dances and drama.

Together, combining these performing arts allows me to use them to express an interpretation of our cycle of living.

Each 'Ogma's Tale Of The Trees' story poem, I share today, is a wandering collage of my own autobiographical and fanciful memories combined with mythology that has inspired me. I include lines of classic poets that I enjoy that seem fitting.

Into all this is an integration of tunes, words, and songs by Claire Roche and her harps. Some of these weave some of her interpretations into the themes of these 20 story poems.

Ogma's Tale Of The Trees, therefore, is a personal expression of the 20 Keys of this woodland based mythology that became Ogma's inspiration for creating the Ogham alphabet.

As I mentioned, these are told and shared as
our Four Seasons.
In a theatre setting, this would probably be known as Four Acts,

Our First Season - our Spring
 ... growth, our new shoots, discovering ourselves
Our Second Season - our Summer
 ... blossoming, connecting
Our Third Season - our Autumn
 ... our harvest, our unity
Our Fourth Season - our Winter
 ... sharing, our divine service

Together they are expressed to interpret living as a cycle rather than a linear beginning to end.

Also expressed is the concept that questions are not for answering but for living within.

 I invite listeners to consider living with questions so that living is a constant exploration of wonder.

Is this Truth or Fiction? ...

Folks often ask me about the history and facts behind some of the things I present through Ogma's Tale Of The Trees. Though a lot of personal experiences are weaved into this work along with archived scribed information too, my Ogma's Tale Of The Trees is a work of fiction. However, I believe that this fiction is also full of truths that may be hard to find in non-fiction scholarly books.

I hope you enjoy exploring, be entertained and inspired by 'Ogma's Tale of The Trees' ...

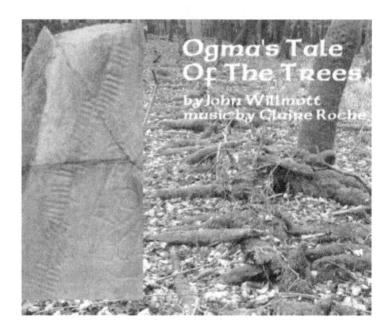

Beith the Birch :

birthing

first life and bringer of life onto this earth

sounding the first note of the first aicme
first note of our Budding and Blossoming Spring

Bathing In The Fae's Breath

Beith The Birch, was the first life on this earth
born here from another world, they say.

From this first birch
all trees,
all plants,
all animals
and ourselves
were served the first breath of life.

As all life comes from a womb somewhere,
the womb, a fire of flames that dances,
warms and glows,
when branches of the birch fuel its hearth,
unconditionally, without fear.

Coleridge tells of the Birch being the
Lady Of The Wood;
but I believe the birch is a man,
a defender and protector of women.

Should any women be abused by a man,
then the birch will punish and inflict
the burning of beating from
its branches upon him.

And this still awaits men in
parts of this world today,
when they challenge the sacred way of women.

Beith the Birch

We had a storm,
a birch fell;
lifeless ivory that spread across the grass.

Lifting its skin, its pink flesh revealed
green lichen still alive, eager to continue.

Later, I wrote a letter,
about the wisdom of this tree
on white pulp from the life of this fallen birch.

While composing this letter I pondered
about how some folks ask
to leave this world for awhile
and then return to begin over.

Fate may sometimes grant what we wish
and snatch us away,
but we do not know of our return.

Earth is a place for love,
I don't know where it's likely to be better,
but if you climb a birch tree ...
You will think you are escaping to heaven,
only to find its branches dip down
to return you safely to earth.

Bathing In The Fae's Breath

For a moment
you do actually leave this earth,
and then you return to start again.

Birch the first life, is the first dance,
and only from that first dance can love begin;
a love that pours this cauldron that
has released this Tale Of The Trees.

some mythology of Beith the Birch ...

I have used mythology I learned through a story that tells of the Birch being the first life on this earth, born from the other world, they say.

This story tells of all trees, all plants, all animals and ourselves, all being born from the same Divine womb, that I will call the 'Mór na Coire Ciúin' through these Ogma's Tale Of The Trees.

Bards have shared stories of Beith the Birch being the defender and protector of women.

They have told of Birch trees standing guard to protect the arrival of all life into this earth,
life that comes from the hearth fire of the Mór na Coire Ciúin.

Bards have also related stories advising that should any women be abused by any man then the Birch will punish him with a beating from its branches. This is still within the law in some countries today, including the Isle of Man.

about my Beith the Birch story poem ...

My story poem has unfolded as a collage of three story visions.

The first vision is of the Birch being the "first life on earth". This is taken from a local story I tell to visitors to Carrowcrory about the 'Birth of Bhride'.

Most people visiting us seem to be more familiar with Brighid than Bhride, but it is the same mythology. In several stories, I also call her Brí na Sióga, or Brí de Óg.

For the first vision, of this story, I strongly express the Birch as being the protector of women.

Lads, do not feel cast aside. You get your turn through the next poem of Luis The Rowan :-) .

The second story vision here flows into an imagery of me speaking through the eyes of Ogma. I am interpreting him as one of the first scribes that came to Erin.

We are told, through stories, that these scribes brought their stories and scribing craft to Erin from the Middle East, and even from Eden itself.

In this second story vision, Ogma approaches a fallen Birch tree and discovers that it is easy to scribe clearly onto its thin bark.

It seems Ogma believes that his scribing regenerates new life into this fallen Birch tree. He believes that his stories, his teachings, and his discoveries, will live on and never be forgotten.

The third story vision here is a reflection of a memory of my son, Holly, who loved, and still loves, to climb trees, without fear. He has had this passion since he was four years old.

I remember him crawling up a trunk of a coppiced Birch tree when its young trunks are very flexible. The higher he climbed, the lower the tree branch would bend to return him back nearer to the ground again … and he was not amused by his lack of progress towards the sky'.

With these three visions together, I am attempting to illustrate our reactions when we indulge in our first experiences. I believe that the outcomes of our first experiences, when we dare to follow our sense of wonder, does sculpture our identity.

We discover who we are, and what our place is in this world.

Luis the Rowan :
loving

discovery of passion, discovery of love

sounding the second note of the first aicme
second note of our Budding and Blossoming Spring

Luis the Rowan

Ogma was walking through the banqueting hall
when an air of sweet harp music
lulled him away from his senses.

When he awoke
a branch of rowan was beside him
with white blossoms on it.

Later, he was attending court
and took the branch of rowan
that he placed into the gathering fire.

The fragrance of the blossom
entered the lungs and the blood
of the hearts of all men present.

And from that gathering fire
a beautiful women appeared
and radiantly poured light upon them all.

Gently she spoke
as white bronze formed beneath her feet
and the court of today's warriors
and tomorrow's heroes
became a home of kindness toward her.

Bathing In The Fae's Breath

And there a tall rowan tree
that had always been barren
filled its branches with flowers,
and on these branches birds gathered
and shared melody that was infectious.

The warriors became enchanted
by the chants of women around them,
in harmony with the strings of harps,
woven into the bows of rowan branches,
releasing sounds wafting
from cauldrons of willow,
attached to the bows of rowan,
that were strung together with bronze.

Within this circle of men in court
there is now no grief,
no gripe, no treason.

Away is the favoured haunt of pleasure!

No taunt, no threat, no maladdiction
when this sweet music
embraces their ears.

No visions of death, no mourning, no sorrow.

Luis the Rowan

Instead, strength, passion and wisdom
embraces all horned feelings
within the court circle.

Inspiring wonder where once was comparison;
Tolerance where once was challenge;
Clear vision where once was mist.

As a dragon's fire ignites in every heart,
and every dragon's tale
is always umbilically connected
to the heart of this one beautiful woman,
in the gathering fire,

The same beautiful woman
that resides, courts and judges
at the point where our two worlds meet.

So there we were,
after the sun had set,
drinking the finest of wines.

Horses of gold ran around us
so we feel our abundance.
Horses of purple ran around us
so we feel our pride as if we are royal.
Horses of blue ran around us
so we feel courage,

Bathing In The Fae's Breath

... and not be restricted
by boundaries of concern for distance and time.

Then into the dawn of new day
the pure man from the bed of the Morrigu
the pure man whose darkness is shed.

With a voice that is no longer
of grief, of slavery, of mourning
but of pure voice from the women of the rowan.

The woman of the rowan
who urged Ogma to make a ship
from her branches
to journey west and always be in a land of joy.

Its not to every man
that this offer made by her.

And so Ogma's journey,
in the rowan boat,
and hoisted sails of salleys,
became another of Ogma's Tale Of The Trees ...

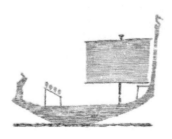

some mythology of Luis the Rowan ...

I have used mythology from a story I was told about the Rowan igniting the fire of the dragon's head that lays in every heart of every living being.

This story tells of the dragon's tail growing longer through each of our ageing cycles while it remains umbilically connected to the Woman Of The Rowan; 'Cí ís Coire Ciúin'. We could say 'Mór na Coire Ciúin', a name that seems to have eventually been shortened to Corran then Rowan.

Direct attempted translation into latinised English of both phrases comes out as nonsense.

'Cí ís Coire an Ciúin' is sort of, 'woman who be the quiet cauldron' or even 'woman who weaves in the valley, or in the cave'.

Is shows that old Gaelic should be understood as it is. Even when it is translated into scribed letters, the interpreted spellings are varied.

'Mór na Coire Ciúin' has been revered through several different names through different traditions.

Around the world this it often known as 'she', and the womb of a goddess that is the mother of all goddesses. Today, the Morrigan, is perhaps the most used name for her.

Bards, through ages, have shared stories of the 'Woman of the Rowan', using one of her names. They speak of her feeding men with spirits of passion, strength, bravery, vision, and focus. Feeding men with the spiritual and emotional 'nourishment,' they require to inspire their destiny, and encourage action and achievement.

These stories have included advising men to burn sticks of Rowan within circles of sanctuary to invite the spirit of this goddess to be present with them. To cloak them, embrace them and ignite their passion and vision, during times of council, court, treaty, and alas, during times of declaring battle.

I find these stories remind us that under every Rowan berry fruit there is the image of the Star of Creation. Legend passed down tells us this is to confirm that the goddess spirit is always present throughout the Rowan tree.

about my Luis the Rowan story poem ...

A lot of mythology is weaved into this story poem.

I believe this poem is quite an Aisling, so I will attempt to reveal some of its visions to you.
Please interpret these as you feel guided.

The main location that inspired this story poem is The Hill Of Tara, as I imagine it when Cormac mac Airt was the high king ruling from there.

From stories I have been told, it appears that this was a time when huge celebrations for Samhain were hosted at Tara every three years.

These celebrations are said to have been the way to bring about unity among all of the chieftains around Erin.

Some stories tell of the main celebration being within a huge Banqueting Hall built on the long cursor that is still seen at the Hill Of Tara.

The finale of each triennial celebration was the burning down of the Banqueting Hall, which would be re-built for the next Samhain gathering event three years later.

Stories also tell of circular courts being held in session around the Hill Of Tara. These were hosted by clan chieftains before they could join the overall unifying celebrations.

Remains of the henges of these courts are still visible on the Hill Of Tara today. Rath Grainne is very pronounced, but not as much as the High King's Court, of course.

The big celebration, The Feis, could not happen until all courts had smoothed out all of the current tensions between clans. It seems most tensions were dissolved through trade agreements hat were bonded by arrangements to exchange goods, services, hostages and even marriages.

Within these court circles would be mainly men, or all men, arriving full of anger, longing and other tense emotions. They would express themselves through lust, combat games, and engage in activities to attract attention from others to feel worthy. They would even carry a willingness to break loyalties to fulfil personal longings, even if this fulfilment was to be short lived.

I tell a story poem featuring Ogma as being a person attending one of these courts.

Luis the Rowan

Ogma arrives at the Banqueting Hall where Bards with their harps skillfully perform the Three Strains that enchant joy, sorrow or sleep.

The strain of melancholy, the 'Goltrai',
that brings about weeping.

The strain of joy, the 'Geantrai',
that brings about laughter and 'mirth'.

The strain of sleeping, the 'Suantrai',
that brings about dreaming.

At the end of each of these words is 'trai', pronounced 'tree', that means 'enchanter'.

... and, here, they do send Ogma to sleep.

Suantrai, the 'strain of sleep' sending Ogma into the Dreaming, the Aisling.

For the rest of this story poem, I invite you to decide for yourself whether Ogma did awake, or at what point he did awake. Or was all of this story within his Dreaming, his Aisling?

We are now introduced to the Rowan ...

From this point I have drawn on stories from our local Céis Coarran, the highest point in Co. Sligo, and it's relationship between harps and Rowan wood. This may not seem clear in this poem, but the relationship between the two is truly there.

High King Cormac mac Airt was born below Céis Coarran here in Co. Sligo. Céis Coarran is one of the current anglicized interpretations of ...
Cí ís Coire an Ciúin

A well told epic legend of here is the story of Diarmuid and Grainne, daughter of Cormac.

I do believe that his daughter, Grainne, did return to this home of her father.

What intrigues me are lesser known stories about Grainne and her life around Céis Coarran.

For example, some of these lesser told stories of Grainne speak of her returning to the triennial court and banqueting time at Tara.

With stories of Grainne in mind, some Bards called her Áine, I include her being at Tara with unseen feminine spirits accompanying her.

This story poem now truly enters into an Aisling as the leading goddess spirit, name not given, enters a circle of the men in court. As the scent of the Rowan blossom enchants the men present we may wonder who or what this woman spirit is, as she connects with them? As these men become enchanted, they see the image of a woman raise from the fire.

At this point, it is up to the reader, or listener, to decide if this is an image of Morrigu, more commonly known as Morrigan, less known as Mór na Coire Ciúin. Or is this Bhride or Brighid rising, or even Grainne or Áine?.

The white bronze at her feet has a similar symbolism as gold, a symbolism of the feminine spirit being fully present.

The men also become aware of several female spirits around them. This distraction causes them to ignore a nearby Rowan tree that breaks into blossom as the women spirits arrive. The voices and chants of women present are also in tune with the drones of the gathering union of harps.

The harps are played by Bards who are all men. Their harps are made from frames of Rowan wood and their sound boxes made from Willow.

The enchantment of the women spirits present, combined with the music from the harps, dissolves away the anger within all of the men present. It dissolves their anxieties, concerns, and longings. The men fully embrace their connection to the feminine spirit.

Celebration of this union and spiritual copulation is celebrated by a vision of horse symbols that appear when passion, confidence and sensory warrior spirit of the men is restored.

When the new morning dawn arrives, each man is awoken with an invitation to confidently and clearly take on a quest.

With all that I have written in this story poem, it is entirely based on one very simple proverb that is shared all around the world.

That is, that behind every successful man ... is a good woman :-)

I have since read the stories of the Voyage Of Bran and see they are quite similar.

Fearn the Alder :

sensing

discovering how our senses respond to elements

sounding the third note of the first aicme
third note of our Budding and Blossoming Spring

Bathing In The Fae's Breath

If, when you are walking,
an alder catkin spins in the breeze,
seemingly asking to be caught by your palm,
for a moment you may stop
your struggle to grasp the meaning of all life.

The alder catkin, small,
falling towards your palm,
weightless as a feather,
only to be blown away by the breeze
before it touches your palm

and then all thoughts about life,
your life and its significance, changes instantly.

What can we change in the world
when in a flash the world can change us.
Where destiny is not our future
but its where our present takes us.

As we sail into new journeys,
if we allow this,
sometimes we don't notice
our compass and co-ordinates changing.

We can awake some mornings
feeling adrift, as castaways;
and then the warm sun on our face
feeds us a breakfast of hope.

Fearn the Alder

Fearn the Alder loves to live beside water.
Fearn the Alder is nourished by water.

It is here it connects with the four elements
as an axis, as a totem,
conducting the orchestra of
water, fire, air and earth.

Ravens, perch on the tallest alders,
raise their black feathers into the awakening sun,
and through their feathers reveal purple,
the royal colour, released only onto the alders.

Erc The Deravid cut a branch from an alder,
and hollowed out a whistle,
and called upon the wind
to spread harmony.

Erc cut another branch,
smouldered it,
to create charcoal of intense heat,
to perform alchemy of metals.

Erc planted seeds of healing herbs,
around the alder trunk,
and the alder's roots released food,
to feed the new born plants
sprouting from these seeds.

Bathing In The Fae's Breath

Erc invited visitors into the water,
beside the alders,
and called upon their spirit guardians
to guide them. And he blessed them.

Here a new child, forever new child,
to dance with the four elements .

A new child, like any of us,
is blessed to dance with the elements,
or choose to command them

Forgive that what we choose may not be the choice
of the falling catkin.

some mythology of Fearn the Alder ...

I have used mythology from a story I learned that tells of an Alder tree conducting the four elements of earth, air, fire, and water. Through doing so, the Alder tree creates an orchestrated alchemy that touches and enlivens our senses.

Bards, through the ages, have shared stories of the spirit of Fearn, the Alder, offering us the choice of living our lives by dancing with the elements. Alternatively, our choice is to be challenged by their alchemy and then live with the consequences that our actions may cause.

Stories have been told of how ancient men of wisdom followed ravens that guided them. Some native totems are made from Alder wood, and include a carved raven on top of them.

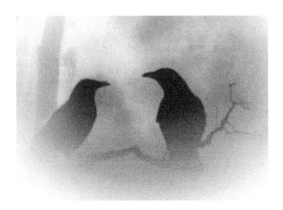

about my Fearn the Alder story poem ...

This story poem started from my memory of an early spring walk through Lough Key Forest Park in Co. Roscommon. It was a windy day and Alder catkins were falling from Alder branches. I was trying to catch them, with some difficulty.

This reminded me of our lessons of how most things do not turn out as we intend or wish for. To command situations and demand that people give their service to our intentions is always a huge challenge. Such requests often return disturbing and upsetting consequences, because our expectations from others have failed.

I first speak of ravens. I notice that when ravens land on high Alder branches they often raise their wings as if they are getting ready to orchestrate the elements.

At this point I introduce the reader, or listener, to Erc The Deravid, a wise man, I believe, that is featured in some of my stories. Erc is a man that I am reluctant to call a priest, druid, shaman or similar because ... he is who he is.

I was first inspired by Erc The Deravid through a story of Saint Brendan, one of the 12 Apostles Of

Ireland. This story told of Saint Brendan being 'schooled' by Céile Dé priests who brought Psalms, Scribing, and the Christ Heart traditions to Erin, and taught them here.

Brendan is well known through the story of his sea voyage to the Americas in a leather boat that included a stop off at Hy Brasil.

Brendan was ordained as a priest by an Erc The Deravid. In this story poem, I have Erc making practical use of the Alder tree as ways to work with each of the four elements.

Erc reminds us that we always have choices, at any time, to flow with the elements or try to command them, but to accept and handle the consequences when we do choose to command them.

Bathing In The Fae's Breath

Saille the Willow :

balancing

experiencing the ebbs and flows of sorrow and joy

sounding the fourth note of the first aicme
fourth note of our Budding and Blossoming Spring

Saille the Willow

Salleys, the willows,
the conduit between the moon and water
and percussion of the tides of life.

The ebbs peaking to touch both worlds
at Samhain and Solmain,
a time now called Bealtaine;

The two times of the year
when the salmon fish
challenge the upstream.

Then relaxing to the flows at each equinox
when our wisdom of change must be our own.

A flow time when no salley leaf
has been born yet
… but is eager to be.

A flow time when no salley leaf has fallen,
but is embraced by the sun
and is called upon to join
the regenerating earth once more.

Salleys tease childhood fancies
and enchant our waking dreams
as we pass by.

Bathing In The Fae's Breath

Salleys speak to us.
Its why harp makers make
sound boxes from them.

We weave salleys
to weave in our wishes and prayers
to be released at the ebbs
... of the meeting worlds.

We wear salleys
to attract friendship and love,
that graft us to an instinct of honour,

So salleys please breathe on us.
It was to here that your spirit guided us.
To here where our names are blessed upon us.
To here where the water you share baptises us.

To here where you charm us
into accepting who we are
and who we will become.

Saille the Willow

some mythology of Saille the Willow ...

I have used mythology from a story that tells of the Willow being a conduit between the moon and water while being the centre of the ebbs and flows of the tides of life.

This story tells of these ebbs and flows peaking at Beltaine and Samhain, the two times of the year when the salmon fish challenge the upstream.

Bards, through the ages, have shared stories of how the spirit of Saille, the Willow, serves us the names that we carry during our time on this world for others to identify us by.

They have told us that our names should be 'confirmed' through us being blessed by water flowing beside Willow trees and under the light of the moon.

Their stories have also been told, as parables, to explain how naming is performed upon us.

Our names, they say, are bonded to us to serve as an inspiration to remind us, and others, about our vision, our destiny, and our place among all things on this earth.

Long ago, our names changed through each rite of living we passed through. That barely happens with most people now. With most of us, the names we are given at birth is what we keep.

about my Saille the Willow story poem ...

With this story poem, I have served a fairly straight presentation of mythology of Willow. I commence with the Willow's association with the moon and water and the ebbs and flows of our life and all life.

I then move through some of the ways we use Willow wood.

I complete this poem by asking the Willow to bless us with our rightful names so we can live according to who we are and what we do on the land that supports us between the moon and the water.

Nuin the Ash :

accepting

learning tolerance and forgiveness

sounding the fifth note of the first aicme
fifth note of our Budding and Blossoming Spring

Bathing In The Fae's Breath

We yearn for sacred circles.
Circles where nothing harms us
when we enter them.

Sanctuary circles, where within them,
there is no more bias, no more conflict
and no more demands to take more from us.

Forgiveness is the way,
speaks Nuin The Ash.
A sailor of the sea of life
tormented by unpredictable swelling seas
and unpredictable calmness of the seas.

A sailor of the sea of life
nourished with fear
that has constipated his whole being.

Became a castaway
from his sunken temple ship
sunken outside of where ash trees circled.

Swellings throughout his body
of fluids, fire, excrement and wind
not knowing where to flow for calm.

Swellings exposing his flag
of his singular priesthood of damnation
for the offered gift of guided destiny.

Nuin the Ash

Circling the ash trees
no matter where he was'

They were pointing, pointing, pointing.
His swellings swirling, swirling swirling.

The castaway circled and circled
outside the circle of the Nuins, the ashes.

But as he circled,
his weakness made him slower and slower.

The slower he moved
a sweetness of fragrance teased him.

A fragrance of sweetness
that became stronger the slower he moved;

Beckoning him to enter the circle
to feed, be nourished and be at home.

some mythology of Nuin the Ash ...

I have used mythology from a story that tells of the Ash commanding the spirit of balance through awareness, through Presence.

Bards, through the ages, have shared stories describing how Nuin the Ash's branches point to points where people should gather. Their stories speak of circles of Ash trees being perfect for forming sacred circles.

Stories have also been told about how conflicts have been solved and dissolved within sacred circles. These are spaces where tolerance is the behaviour and forgiveness is the way.

Can these stories guide us to know how and where to find our truth? When we find that place and surrender to it, can we call that place our 'home'?

The pic on the previous page is of the David Nash living sculpture, Ash Dome, at his Tremenheere Gardens in North Wales, well worth a visit.

Nuin the Ash

about my Nuin the Ash story poem ...

I commence this story poem with a reference to our desire for 'sacred circles'.

Sacred circles could be symbolic of several places but with this story the journey is to discover that place where we truly feel we belong, connected, and loved.

Before this discovery happens, I move this story through how we are tormented by fear of the unknown, mistrust of people, and nervous of situations. I include our possible blurred vision of our worthiness for love and connection.

I also aim to express our anguish when we try to find that special place that is "exactly" what we feel we need. This anguish includes keeping a distance away from people, places and situations and avoid all contact. I express this as a prolonged dark flow of suffering imagery, so this story poem reveals itself as one of my darker stories.

This story poem is intended to be about our transition between our individuality that has matured from self-discovery, into our willingness to share ourselves.

This story poem leads into our attempts at connecting who we are with what we are willing to share with others. The surprise we may experience is the inner releasing of relief and calm. This is made possible through tolerance and forgiveness when we do truly connect with others.

We discover that our intolerance only casts us away back out to sea again. Intolerance and unforgiveness casts us away to remain as weather tormented barren islands ... Home is where we can balance being with others and accept the changing elements ... all without longings.

Huathe the Hawthorn :

mating

flirting, courting, and mischief

sounding the first note of the second aicme
first note of our Fruiting Summer

Bathing In The Fae's Breath

Huathe the Hawthorn plays mischievous trickery
if we attempt to define what is real and unreal,
until we discover its not a question
of how to live,
but it's the question that is our life.

Huathe the Hawthorn is full of riddles
Lures us, embraces us, then it hides.
Fragrances flirt within wombs of women,
triggering sparks of lustful longing ...
... of men to join them in a mating dance.

From the circles and swirling of dance;
Dances of wonder, hoping and lust.
Huathe pulls away the blanket of time,
a tease of the faerie folk, they say.

A tease of the faerie folk?
Some ask around hearth fires
that cackle when stoked
with a thorn twig or two.

My fire is lit.
My bed is made
of hawthorn flowers gathered.
I'm far away from any home.

Huathe the Hawthorn

She came to me.
Night time, moon time,
in the spring-time,
under the starlight,
beneath a hawthorn tree.

She trod softly
over the new ferns and shamrock
towards my white chamber,
towards my sweet bed,
to rest her warm breast with me,
beneath the hawthorn tree.

I had always thought, I had always been told,
Not to touch hawthorns I'll forsake luck;
That a soul may pass from this earth early,
That the water will stop flowing
throughout the land.

But there something I feel, before I'm too old,
I must lay with the hawthorn
where I will bless hope,
and heal a broken heart.

Nobody knows who seeds a hawthorn tree,
what sprouts its warning thorn,
what scents its embracing blossom.
We know it came long ago.

Hawthorne hands gripped into the earth
while our eyes glanced towards the sky.

some mythology of Huathe the Hawthorn ...

I have used mythology from a story that tells of the Hawthorne encouraging us to play with others. I believe that whenever we play, through mischief and flirting, we enter into a dance of discovery.

Bards, through the ages, have shared stories of the mischievous spirit of Huathe, the Hawthorn, in May, the start of summer.

This is the time when Hawthorn blossom releases subtle fragrances that flirts with the wombs of women and ignites sparks of lustful longing.

about my Huathe the Hawthorn story poem ...

My story poem here opens up the second quarter of the year. This is the time when budding spring flows into blossoming summer.

We enthusiastically present invitations to others to share some fun. Connecting and sharing with other people becomes a quest to adventure into the unknown. Sending invitations is often followed by moments of uncertainty when we question what will flow from what we do together.

I do not start this story poem with a cautious handshake or a warming healing hug, but with a bit of a touchy-feely, flirting, mischief. We youthfully engage in a mating dance of wonder.

We float aimlessly and cautiously when we manoeuvre around these new feelings. We juggle with feelings that lure us to connect with new people. We may call these temptations. We may blame these feelings on the spells of Faerie Folk that bring boys and girls together.

This story poem opens with innocent feelings blending into dance and drama as part of playful May time. May traditions today still include Hawthorn May Trees and their blossoms.

The poem changes into a slower mood that moves into intimate moments of mating in May. We are brought to a hidden bed within the forest, that is prepared with Hawthorn blossoms, for the mating meeting after the Bealtaine 'Hunt'.

Words towards the end speak, "I will bless hope and heal a broken heart".

This is not referring to a past or lost human relationship. This sentiment reveals that any hurt from a romance lost is never the crisis we think it is. When we may feel our ego is totally crushed, it is a reminder that something wonderful is about to happen.

The last two lines, of this story poem, may not seem to make sense, and they are not intended to be grammatically correct. These lines express the connection of worlds at the moment when a couple consummate and join life together.

This is a moment that I find is impossible to put into methodical words and grammar, because if I could, I feel such words could never be true.

𝒟𝓊𝒾𝓇 𝓉𝒽𝑒 𝒪𝒶𝓀 :

accountability

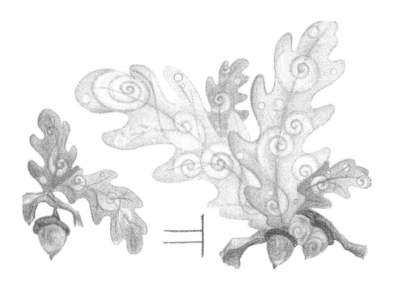

being present to all things around us at all times

sounding the second note of the second aicme
second note of our Fruiting Summer

Bathing In The Fae's Breath

Oh mighty oak how bold you stand
stretching your limbs to
bless this wondrous land.
Roots dug deep, branches like arms,
Leaves like hands, sanctuary to calm.

The oak invites sanctuary to rest and to think.
We know many men have passed this way,
within this tree their spirits are here
to share with us today.
Children sometimes come to play.
tie a swing onto a branch,
or dream of their future
to idle a summer away.

Come back here often with friends, with lovers,
as mothers, as grandfathers
to dream of more futures,
until our last days.

Believing the oak judges our every move.
answers our questions,
an oracle that speaks, our proof.
Each spring arms stretch wider.
New green leaves are greener.
Once again new sap runs through it's veins,

Duir the Oak

Who rides by? Who stops to rest?
Who seeks judgement here;
seeking the key to turn the lock
of their prison door and be told,
it's ok, you are free?

And what if someone to be judged rides by,
First to hunt a deer,
Riding abreast their soul, galloping,
breaking it in, bringing it to calm,
to release its mortal fear.

After a thoughtful, blessed,
calm, loving summer,
a mighty wind blew night and day.

They call it fall.
It stole the oak's leaves away.
It snapped its branches, tugged at its bark.
The oak became tired now looking stark.

The waning oak tree breathed
and tightly gripped the ground;
standing firm and stubborn,
while other trees fell all around.

The wind also getting weary
panted and whispered,
"How can you still be standing Oak?"

Bathing In The Fae's Breath

The oak tree took a breath and spoke
You may break a branch or two,
scare every leaf to fall away,
shake my trunk and make me sway.

My arms may seem weak.
My trunk start to creak.
But my roots are deep down
where you can't see
the deepest part of me,
the strongest part of me.

In spring those who come to rest here
ask me how much more of life can they endure.
I whisper to them how much I can endure.

What I have discovered, thanks to you,
makes me, the wise oak they say,
stronger than I ever knew.

To those who rest here I request this
discover the joy of planting a tree.
Watch it rise, its slow I know.

Watch it rise, branches wanting
to touch the skies,
then learning to point
east, west, south and brave the north.

Duir the Oak

As it grows, so will your adoration of life,
your bigger warmer heart
waxing with each spring.

Yes, there's nothing like planting a tree!
That joy is quite a thing,
especially when it sings
to converse with the winds and birds.

Oh mighty oak, how bold you stand
for hundreds of years on this challenged land;
reminding us there is beauty, singing birds,
and your giving of shelter and shade.

I wish to be like an oak tree
planted by the rivers of the water of life,
abundant with fruit when it is in season,
when leaves may fall knowing
new buds are here too.

Proving that through whatever we do
... we shall prosper.

some mythology of Duir the Oak ...

I have used mythology that tells of the Oak being a tree of prophecy. It tells of Duir, the Oak, being connected to an unseen archive of all that has been and will be.

Bards, through the ages, have shared stories of Duir the Oak being the judge of what spirit is 'charged' into our new human bodies before birth.

Through stories, they tell of the spirit of the Oak as being the 'all knowing'. It being aware of our time to arrive on this Earth, and of the time when we are to leave.

Some bards proclaim Duir the Oak, the seventh tree, is truly the "Tree Of Life", and neither the Ash tree, or Apple tree of some traditions.

Some people may quietly seek for their ancestors through the Oak ...
... while others may seek contact with those who have not arrived here yet.

Bardic stories speak of the Oak being the 'guardian' that inspires our loving care of the 'garden' of where we live, and all that grows and lives around us.

about my Duir the Oak story poem ...

I start this story poem with a verse from a song I wrote while sitting by an Oak when I was 14 years old. The second verse is recent writing. It reflects on that time when I wrote the first verse. I continue with snippets of observations of people I see and meet in the forests.

I enjoy watching people in the woods. I enjoy their reactions from play, and discovery. People of several generations of ages are in the forest. Many of them stop for a moment by an Oak tree as if they feel that the Oak is watching them, and judging what is happening.

My story poem then enters surreal thoughts that compare judgement and accountability with our desires to be free of all concerns. We are always haunted by a caution of wondering whether what we are doing with and for others is right or wrong.

This story poem then twists into a story of an Oak tree's strength and determination through a strong windy storm. Survival of the Oak is portrayed as accepting the challenges that each moment serves us and also trusting our reactions.

This is about facing survival without a need to answer questions and without consideration of consequences. It is about survival through trust.

When winter has passed, the story poem speaks of people returning to the Oak tree to confess and share their stories of how they passed through winter. But no matter what they share, none of their experiences were as fierce as what the Oak had endured through the winter.

Through this writing, I question which is the most most honest form of judgement? Is judgement formed from personal experience and accumulated personal wisdom?

The Oak tree's advice is to plant an Oak sapling, watch it grow, and learn from its challenges as it grows steady and strong.

This story tells of watching an Oak tree grow as an inspiration for us to replace our questions of "what if" with "what is". Through doing so, the Oak could teach us to grow our adoration of life rather than grow a fear of it.

Then, I finish with the last verse of the song that I wrote while I sat against the Oak trunk, when I was only 14 years old.

Tinne the Holly :

courage

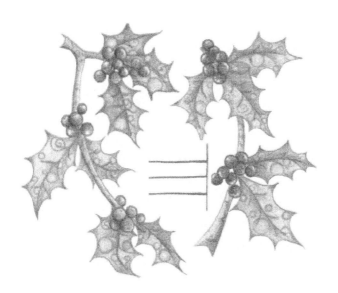

**having courage to be honest
with affirmations and prayers**

*sounding the third note of the second aicme
third note of our Fruiting Summer*

Bathing In The Fae's Breath

Glossy leaves wrinkled and reaching,
Antennas that guide curious eyes,
Seeing and seeking to moralize
A path of wisdom.

Gentle with all I seek to be.
Gentle with holly I desire to be.
At home amid my friends I wish be,
Instead of sitting on thorns of solitude.

When glassy eyes gaze on glossy leaves,
Tinne the Holly lifts us from melancholy.
It removes darkness from thoughts.
It shines its light though our face to our soul.

Messages of our prayers are lifted,
Delivered to that place
We ponder but never picture.
The reply is the blessing, love,
and abundance we deserve.

Green groweth the holly,
So doth the ivy.
When flowers cannot be seen,
And greenwood leaves be gone,

Tinne the Holly

Blow, blow, thou winter wind,
Thou art not so unkind.
Not so demanding
As man's ingratitude.

Heigh ho, sing heigh ho,
Unto the green holly.
Yes, heigh ho for the holly!
This life is most jolly.

Freeze, freeze, thou bitter sky,
Thy sting is not so sharp.
As friend remember'd not.
Sing heigh ho for the holly:

Is loving mere folly?
Are memories melancholy?
Sing heigh ho for the holly!
Who says life is most jolly.

verse five is from a poem by Henry VIII,
'Green Groweth The Holly'
and the last four verses are from
William Shakespeare's
'Blow, Blow Thy Winter Wind' poem ...

some mythology of Tinne the Holly ...

I have used mythology that tells of the spirit of Holly being the carrier of our prayers. These are prayers that go to the place we cannot name but may try to give a name to.

This mythology also tells that these prayers return to us carrying blessings, love, light and abundance to serve us what we deserve.

Bards, through the ages, have told stories of the spirit of Tinne, the Holly, raising us from empty melancholy by removing thick darkness from our thoughts and allowing light to shine through.

Some ancient tales compare how, through winter, the Holly tree shows off its green during this time when the nearby Oak is without leaves ... but in summer Holly hides within the dome of the Oak's abundance of green leaves.

Tinne the Holly

about my Tinne the Holly story poem ...

Sometimes, I deliberately add a few lines from classic poets into my story poems. In this story poem, I have included some lines from King Henry VIII of England. I did this in response to finding myself attempting to write this story poem in Tudor times poetry style. Why I did this, I am still not sure. There are four verses from William Shakespeare here too.

Through the first verse of this poem, I am curious about what visions will come to me from my mindfulness of the Holly. This verse was written spontaneously as a doodle. It took awhile for the rest of the words and verses to flow from me.

What eventually came to me was a realization that I had been working alone for awhile. At that time, I was totally focused on trying to achieve my goals and dreams. A day came when I realized it was time to lighten up, and share some fun time with other people again.

To wrap up my time of solitude I let go of my goals and let loose some prayers to be delivered to that unseen place where dreams are received and responded to.

Through this story poem, I remind how the Holly tree is seen at its best through winter. This is the time when the leaves of other trees are not there to hide the Holly.

I suggest that perhaps, like the Holly, we should be more seen in winter too? By doing so, it could prevent winter melancholy infecting us. I feel that when we are without melancholy no wind can harm or chill us. No cold people can hold us back. We just continue to be jolly.

The last four verses of this story poem, written by Shakespeare, celebrates the joy of having fun with others, together.

Coll the Hazel :

nourishing

giving and receiving nourishment beyond food

**sounding the fourth note of the second aicme
fourth note of our Fruiting Summer**

Breathing In The Fae's Breath

In a wise diviner's hand,
The forked hazel stretched apart.
Feeling, sensing
what's beneath our vibrant land.
Sensing living waters carving an alignment chart
Of its flow from the divine earthly heart.

Hazel-wand tracing the thread of the veil,
Guiding, the diviner's trust as it casts its spell.
We pass slowly, silently though this dara vale,
Trusting, anticipating, this old ways miracle;
Finding that point
where the living waters becomes a well.

Hazel is of a mercurial spirit
A wise sprite, bringer of insight.
Flashes of inspiration,
invites us to discover many things.

Entering into the dreaming within the forest,
A hazel tree sang to me,
Touched me with its fragrant fingers,
Stroking my dream, calming my dream,
Closing the wounds of blood
that had clouded my dream

Breathing air, touched by the hazel,
Charged with quicksilver energy,
Charging me with exhilaration and inspiration.

Coll the Hazel

Hazel charged my spirit to pulsate,
A catalyst, a transformer,
a bard to relate,
Ways to crack any situation,
Like cracking a hazel nut shell
To feed from its nourishment inside.

Pure nourishment,
Pure goodness,
Pure knowledge,
In a nutshell,
All of the ways of wisdom,
we can pass on.

I was now the diviner,
I had discovered my source
Of language, poetry,
And music, of course.

Mystics say anyone born
under the sign of the hazel
must never hoard their treasure.
Its nuts, the fruits of knowledge,
Must be shared
for learning and for pleasure .

Play with the thoughts and dreams of others
From social causes,
to capricious lovers,
But be careful ...
word wizardry can cut!
Remember, your wisdom is inspired by a nut.

some mythology of Coll the Hazel ...

I have used mythology that suggests that the nuts of the Hazel trees are sacred nutrition for the Salmon of Knowledge.

Bards, through the ages, have shared stories of Coll the Hazel's nuts being the food source to nourish us towards enlightened wisdom.

This suggests that Hazel nuts must have served as an essential food of bards. Bard food for grasping wisdom from inspiration and to provide energy through their enduring travels. From hazel nuts, Bards receive the energy they need so they can share their wisdom through rhymes and tunes.

Coll the Hazel

about my Coll the Hazel story poem ...

The first two verses of this story poem are a dedication to my late Uncle Cecil. When I was very young, he used to share Sunday bicycle rides with me to explore megalithic remains that I spotted and plotted from Ordnance Survey maps.

My Uncle Cecil also loved woods and trees. Among the trees, near the ancient sites we visited, he would seek out Hazel trees and select Hazel twigs to use as divining rods.

With these rods, he would seek outflows of underground water and follow them. Sometimes, he found a fresh water spring, and sometimes these water springs were sacred wells that were covered with wild shrub growth.

As my story poem continues, I break into a few lines reflecting on how some folks align trees to astrological sun signs. With the words I use here I do not reveal the sun sign names but do reveal the metal related to it.

As my sun sign is Virgo, and some astrologers relate this sign to Hazel. I slip into a couple of skippy verses around the two names of Virgo's related metals.

These verses are also there to describe the sensations of holding the divining Hazel twigs.

The story poem moves on to share the experience that carrying Hazel rods had empowered upon me. This was far more than just finding a flow of water to a spring. I try to describe this as an attunement into a flow of the unseen that serves us wisdom, as if this is nourishment too.

I conclude this story poem with a suggestion that personal discoveries of wisdom are not for hoarding for personal satisfaction, personal fame, or recognition. Wisdom is a gift for sharing.

The last few words of the last line give reference to how the Hazel nut is an
incredible source of wisdom nutrition.

Quirt the Apple :

connecting

accepting our inspirations and dreams as our guide

sounding the fifth note of the second aicme
fifth note of our Fruiting Summer

Bathing In The Fae's Breath

Did you know that within every apple there lies
Something waiting to surprise.
Instead of slicing down, slice through,
And watch a star appear and twinkle for you!

At harvest time each day on my ladder,
I reach closer towards the sky,
Picking apples, filling barrels,
for mead, for cider, and to make apple pie.

But I am done with apple-picking for now.
Time for winter sleep that longer nights allow.
The scent of the apples calms me and calls me.
What will my dreaming allow me to be.

In the twilight before sleep
I can see apples appear and disappear;
every one with perfect skin shining clear.
Yes, this was the great harvest we all desired,
To nourish us through winter, but now I'm tired

And there are voices singing,
Apples, apples, look here's our treat,
Big and small they're all good to eat.
One side red, other side green,
Russets and coxes all washed clean.

Quirt the Apple

But where are the crab-apples,
Still out in the wood?
Bitter for the big folk,
But for us they are good!

So come all ye,
Let's gather them up:
Make jelly with honey
And mead for us to sup.

From mead we reveal stories
Of darkness to light;
Monsters who became angels
To guide us through the night.

A poet once visited,
Told us of his longing,
Seeking for the dream,
His desire for courting.

Though I am old with wandering;
Through hollow lands and hilly lands,
I will find out where she has gone,
And kiss her lips and take her hands;

We walked with him among long dappled grass,
And plucked till time and times are done.
The silver apples of the moon,
The golden apples of the sun.

Bathing In The Fae's Breath

Through a moment's smile,
He shared more wisdom for awhile;
Peering above spectacles steamed,
As we giggled, burped and beamed.

This is a tree
With leaves so green.
Here are its apples
That hang in between.

If I picked two apples,
do you know what I would do?

Shine them up,
keep one for me,
give the other one to you.

verses 9 to 12 are satire on 'The Song Of The Wandering Aengus' poem by W.B. Yeats

some mythology of Quirt the Apple ...

I have used mythology that tells of the Apple being the awakener of dreams stored in our souls. Dreams that inspire us with prophecy that we manifest through our awakening days.

Bards, through the ages, have shared stories of Quirt the Apple bearing fragrant blossoms and waxy fruit from which stories of the fae and the sidhe will always be created and told.

They tell us that fairy stories reveal the dark side of our dreams, if we do not accept them, or the light side of dreams if we choose to let our dreams guide us.

Bathing In The Fae's Breath

about my Quirt the Apple story poem ...

There is a bit of whimsy through this story poem.

I commence with a demonstration of how cutting an Apple reveals a five pointed star.

This moves on to introducing an Apple picker who gets tired and falls asleep. As he falls into that slumber zone between waking and sleep, he dreams of sorting Apples. Out of this is heard the voices of "little people", the Fae maybe.

At this point, I slide into being an Apple picker that is within the dream world of William Butler Yeats. This is the 'world' that inspired his poetry.

Though he is not named, W.B.Yeats enters this world to be with the "little people". I venture through an altered version of part of his Song Of The Wandering Aengus poem. The "little people" find W.B. a little bit too serious, so they tease him and encourage him to be more playful.

The theme of this poem is to encourage us to grasp opportunities to exchange fantasies and play together rather than be self absorbed in a hermit world. It asks us to be discovered now, rather than be discovered after we have left this earth.

Muin the Vine :

flowing

**allowing dreams to manifest
in our waking world**

*sounding the first note of the third aicme
first note of our Harvesting Autumn*

Bathing In The Fae's Breath

Wine is the blood
that holds us together,
through storms or drought
its always fair weather.

A man and woman cannot copulate
when airs of strife and hatred holds;
when truth is not naked and still,
unwrapped from fables openly told.

Into our glasses
as essence from those isles afar,
splashes of cinnamon, citrus and oak,
nice legs, they say, forming on our jar.

Together we toast what will unite us from vines.
Waters from our wells that nature combines;
joins together our blood for unity we say.
Water to wine is what joins us today.

Resist gods of winds!
Resist gods of fire!
For with wine its always fair weather
when we are together.

In thy fats our cares be drown'd,
With thy grapes our hairs be crown'd!
Cup us till the world go round,
Cup us and the world will go round!

Muin the Vine

that last verse of the poem are lines from William Shakespeare's Antony and Cleopatra.

some mythology of Muin the Vine ...

There is a mythology story that tells of the Vine being the key to open our dreams so they can manifest into our waking world. Some people define this as "knowledge" while others define this as "wisdom", but what is the difference?

Bards through the ages have shared stories of Muin the Vine being the spirit that receives, filters and re-distributes the unseen. It is the spirit that morphs the unseen into our waking world so that we can see, smell, touch, hear and taste it.

It seems like Muin the Vine, could be the vine of grapes, rosehips or berries. Which fruit it is, we are not sure, but we know they all can be used to make fine wines.

about my Muin the Vine story poem ...

Moving into the Third Quarter now, the symbolism of Muin still holds us on to the dream world inspired by Quirt the Apple. Now, it conducts our dreams into our waking world.

When I think of Muin The Vine, my imagination visualizes intoxication from wine followed by the revealing consequences that we awaken to when we sober up. I decided it would be fun to write a story poem that would follow that path.

The opening two lines are an attempt to be poetic about our belief that having a few bevies will transform us into revealing solutions and a complete knowing of all truths.

The second verse extends this idea that passion may not be possible without a few bevies either, or a few scoops, as some say in Ireland.

Third verse takes us further into the alcohol intoxicated world. Now, we reveal an appreciation for our senses being awoken from the addition of spices within a mulled drink.

Muin the Vine

The words carry on this belief that wine and intoxication are a way to bring us together in trust. Through our trust in others we believe we can make all of our dreams come true.

The climax is a belief that intoxication by wine, or vine, will protect us from all harm. I complete this tale with a verse of Shakespeare from Anthony and Cleopatra ... we know what happened to them.

Overall, this poem is not an attempt at spiritual revelation or even be a carrier of a spiritual message. It is calling for being united with others, and all life, so that we can gather in our 'harvest'.

Perhaps the following story poems are more useful for that. Meanwhile, enjoy the fun here.

Gort the Ivy :

trusting

becoming aware of our unseen spirit guide

sounding the second note of the third aicme
second note of our Harvesting Autumn

Gort the Ivy

from the fourth verse, is my adaption of a Charles Dickens poem, 'The Ivy Green'

Don't let love fade away , and make us all islands,
never charted, never enchanted,
dissolved into the sea, not to be seen again.

Connected invitation, the mankind of creation,
binds us as a nation,
as guests on this world.
Love expectations,
unity celebrations,
faith integrations,
one strong binding love is unfurled.

Oh, a dainty plant is the Ivy green,
that creepeth o'er ruins old!
Fast she stealeth on,
though she wears no wings,

And a staunch old heart has she.
How closely she twineth,
how tight she clings;
sharing love with any willing tree.

Whole ages have fled
and their works decayed,
and nations have scattered been;
but the stout old Ivy shall never fade,

Bathing In The Fae's Breath

From its hale and hearty green,
binding together as king and queen.
Oh, a plant of unity
is the Ivy green.

There are a lot of things we may bond with,
a lot of things to pull us back down.
There maybe tears, maybe pain,
stops our world, 'till we get it spinning again.

A hammer may fall to test our weakness.
A saw may grind to cut us
and make us branchless.
But together there is always a power to heal.

From cold stone
to green leaves of warm feel,
creeping on where time has been;
a rare old plant is the Ivy green.

Gort the Ivy

some mythology of Gort the Ivy ...

I was inspired by mythology that tells of Ivy supporting our spirit that protects us from weakness. This is weakness that may happen when we resist the spirit of love flowing through us.

Bards, through the ages, have shared stories of the spirit of Gort, The Ivy, leading us to understand and relate to our spirit guide, no matter how we describe or name it according to our faith.

about my Gort the Ivy story poem ...

This story opens up to encourage making brave and strong choices when a loved one appears to have left our life, either through passing on or through partnership break up.

Why seclude yourself to mourn for long?

The story then motivates the choice to connect with all things of life and nature, again
... and we are introduced to the Ivy Green, a name from Charles Dickens' writings.

I continue with a couple of longish verses describing how Ivy Green connects to trees and walls.

When Ivy grows and creeps up walls, the lime and mortar breaks away. Ivy pushes its stem roots into the mortar that crumbles and is pushed out.

Unfortunately, this behaviour of Ivy on buildings has caused it to carry a false blame of killing trees that it attaches to. Many people believe Ivy feeds from trees and slowly kill them.

This is far from true. Ivy has its own root feeding system well established in the ground. The Ivy fibres that cling onto trees are only for support and barely dig into tree bark, not even to the first ring.

Some readers may think that this story poem is being metaphoric of people we may fall in love with that seem to bleed our energy to support their own. Many believe this is what Ivy does to trees.

The truth is that Ivy is love and support for a tree. An ailing tree usually lives longer when Ivy clings. Maybe we can 'blame' mistletoe as being more metaphoric of what we suspect Ivy of.

As I read or sing this tale, I find it is symbolic of our unseen guide, spirit guide as many say, that supports us at all times. That unseen guide may also be a soaker of our blame.

Gort the Ivy

Despite things seeming to go wrong, and love seeming to fade away sometimes, the support of Ivy Green never fades. When all seems to stop, the breath of Ivy gets things moving again.

As Dickens says ...
It's a rare old plant, is the Ivy Green.

Bathing In The Fae's Breath

nGetal the Reed :
instinct

**trusting responses
to our affirmations and prayers**

*sounding the third note of the third aicme
third note of our Harvesting Autumn*

nGetal the Reed

Do we remember
what our prayers are for.
Is there purity in our words,
or do we ask for more?
Through what we asked for,
do we believe,
We are truly prepared
for all we will receive.

Together, folded by the night,
we lay on earth. I hear.
From far low words breathe
on my breaking brain.
Come! I yield.
Bend deeper upon me! I am here.
Subduer, do not leave me!
Only joy, only anguish,

Take me, save me,
soothe me, spare me!
As I discover
life is a gift, when we
hold it, share it, bear it,
and use no scripts;
true treasure,
never found on pirate ships.

Bathing In The Fae's Breath

Whenever you feel like
no one is close,
close your eyes
to see who shows
up here to guide you
through this day
and leave the bad news
to yesterday.

Can we pray openly
with fullness of joy?
Can we pray laughing,
eyes open to enjoy?
Pray at moments of need,
or pray as a love spell deed;
Learning that we have to receive
all that is sent by Ngetal the Reed.

A couple of lines in verses two and three taken from 'A Prayer' by James Joyce

some mythology of NGetal the Reed ...

I have used mythology that tells of the Reed being the holder and memory of prayers.

Bards, through the ages, have shared stories of the spirit of Ngetal, the Reed releasing the radiance of prayers and have taught people to craft reeds into symbols of release. They have shared ways of weaving reeds that commit to the purest sanctification of our prayers as we weave..

about my NGetal the Reed story poem ...

Through the first verse of my story poem, I question the honesty that we place into our dreams and how we may interpret them.

The second verse uses words of James Joyce from 'A Prayer at the end of Pomes Penyeach'. To me, it describes an anguish that may suffer when our prayers are not honest, and the responses we receive are distant from what we expected and hoped for.

As the rest of the words unfold, we realize what prayers are for. Prayers become lessons of accepting responses without questions.

Bathing In The Fae's Breath

Straif the Blackthorn :

surrender

**awareness of our egos
and balanced place in all situations**

*sounding the fourth note of the third aicme
fourth note of our Harvesting Autumn*

Straif the Blackthorn

With my blackthorn cane
I prodded and pointed to find my way.
With my fairy tales limb
I was a hero to face giants I needed to slay.
Live blossom scent convinced me
and inspired me where to go;
But nay, those giants were my ancestry
wrapped up in a sloe.

A sloe, or two, with apples
makes mighty fine jelly,
but if not kept dark, cold, and hidden,
may get a bit too smelly.
So left in the cold,
and through any treacherous night,
I stay awake, longing for light,
so I can, at last, taste this delight.

But as soon as
came the morrow,
Eager to commence it
without sorrow,
'She' came sweet, sincere
and most definitely cunning;
'Her' eyes, my eyes joined at the jelly,
that started running .

Bathing In The Fae's Breath

Tears, hot, dropped
from just above my face.
Darkness to light searingly hurt
but, yay, I have found my place.
Beyond all calling to all points
that break us and betray.
Escaped from the gauntlet of all pain
that a hero carries today.

Some say, better the bramble
than the blackthorn;
Better the blackthorn
than the devil re-born.
Because a blackthorn stick.
or flower, guides
us to a place where
there's no need to hide.

But where is this place,
a lone worn traveller may ask?
I say, ask the blackthorn faerie,
but first she will give you a task.
And I warn you she'll mark you
with her berries of indelible ink.
But you'll love all, if you surrender
to the nectar she'll offer you to drink.

some mythology of Straif the Blackthorn ...

I have used mythology that tells of the Blackthorn being the sharer of Omens and that inhalation of Blackthorn scent opens up our awareness to the place of our egos.

Bards, through the ages, have shared stories of the spirit of Straif, the Blackthorn, inspiring how people, animals, trees, and plants respond to the presence of everything around them.

They tell us how finding our place can release us from the shackles of illness, and from good health and perception have revelations revealed.

about my Straif the Blackthorn story poem ...

It is said that if we carry a Blackthorn stave, or stick, we are protected from unseen harm approaching us. It is also said that snakes will not come near us when we carry Blackthorn.

So, with the start of this story poem I stride with confidence believing that nothing will harm me. I get pompous due to an invitation from evil to try and tempt me.

Alas, those we call challenging, and even evil, were part of our ancestry. Therefore they are also part of us now. All of this challenge is symbolized by the sloe berry on the Blackthorn

But there is a way to tame this! Instead of interpreting whatever we shut out as foe, we can befriend. Think of the corrupting bitter tasting sloe berry that can make mighty fine jelly.

Accepting this jelly's sweetness, is like something beautiful becoming visible before us. This beauty and warm embrace could and would never have happened if we did not disarm our Blackthorn stave. This is a test to allow trust to include us, and not be something that revolves around us.

We do not have to be heroes to be loved. We can let love be the hero, our bringer of harvest, bringer of nourishment and founder of trust in unity.

Ruis the Elder :

conscience

**listening to an inner voice
that guides us through choices**

sounding the fifth note of the third aicme
fifth note of our Harvesting Autumn

Bathing In The Fae's Breath

A travelling poet,
called George Borrow,
told me things about Elder
I could borrow;
such as, it holds a witch
within its bark,
always a lovely witch
who haunts the dark.

I'll tell ye a tale of love
for a mortal maid.
She said her bed
was what the faeries had made;
but a fae's omen is always woven
into all they make;
but as a young lad
love was anything I could take.

She thought she had enraptured me
with her charms,
but my thoughts were more
than being wrapped in her arms.
Aye, those were days I may brag
as being young and astray,
but 'twas that bed omen from the Cailleach
was what 'ad 'er way

Ruis the Elder

What I thought was love
had stopped flowing, strewth;
and that mortal maid soon found 'erself
a fairer youth.
But in remorse I was saved by
the witch within the elder's bark;
that lovely forgiving witch,
they say, who haunts the dark.

She asked me for apples,
she asked me for honey,
but not once did she ask me
to count out me money.
The potion she made included
some of her elder too.
I drank it and drank it
believing my passion would renew.

But, not only did my passion get shorter,
my arms and legs did too.
My body turned into sinews
that I could feel the wind blow through.
Arms began to caress me and, yes,
love again began to flow.
I had become a harp ...
and through me love was for all to know.

some mythology of Ruis the Elder ...

I have used mythology that tells of the Elder being the wise Cailleach of the trees being our voice of conscience. She can reveal either the gift of Divine love or fear of something dark behind us.

Bards, through the ages, have shared stories of the spirit of Ruis, the Elder, inspiring us to respond to omens by caring more for all life upon this earth.

They also tell us of curses that may be cast upon us if we try to live by domination rather than by co-ordination with the balancing spirits of nature.

about my Ruis the Elder story poem ...

I start my story poem with some George Burrow poetry as I was reading his Elder Witch poem before sailing off into my own imagination and writing some lines of my own. Some of the first verse and much of the second verse are direct from Burrow's poem.

I wrote this as a reflection of conscience. George Burrow's words helped me along to explain this.

This story poem is inspired by our 'devil vs goodness' conflicts.

These are often portrayed by cartoonists as good and evil bubbles above the head. Here I am, the young lusty man taking advantage of opportunity with a young lass. A voice within me, the voice of the Cailleach of the nearby Elder maybe, caused me to question if my lust was honest and loving or self satisfying trickery.

The result of these thoughts, maybe an omen upon me, stopped my love juices flowing, and alas frustrated the lass I was lusting.

But, my choices changed, guided by an inner voice from the Cailleach. My vision of love changed from lust for lasses to a lust of life and all that is living.

Through the story poem this new conscience, new vision of love, changed the way I looked and the way I appeared. My physical being changed and changed … until I took on the form of a harp, through which all love could flow through, and not just my own personal quest for love.

This becomes a transition taking us from our third quarter of unity and harvest into the fourth quarter of Divine service and sharing.

Bathing In The Fae's Breath

Ailim the Pine :

service

**discovering our true home
from which to serve from**

*sounding the first note of the fourth aicme
first note of our Transforming Winter*

Ailim the Pine

Ailim the Pine
must always find its own home.
A pine planted by human hand
can remain sad, longing and alone.

During our growing we fulfil
our own sense of belonging,
our own feelings,
of being at home.

That personal sanctuary,
our sacred seat,
where every inner particle
become its most complete.

Where our vision and performance
becomes its best;
end of a journey
where we have earned our rest.

And then, for no reason
we can account for,
we carry a dread of a moment
when all of the good moments are gone.

I carried that once, that dread,
and turning west
I saw pines against a whitening sky.
Their dark pointed heads against a quiet sky.

Bathing In The Fae's Breath

There was peace at that moment,
I laughed,
and I was reminded that
good moments do not go away.

Ailim the Pine, lush in all seasons,
allows birds to perch to rest, sing and play.
No angst when they land, no reason;
no pining for their return, when they fly away.

In a heart of a pine tree
there is no apprehension,
no wish to fall,
no wish to sleep and awaken.

Tree groves were the first temples.
Learning the trees of the earth
was simple,
as they wrote poems upon the sky.

Ailim the Pine

Later we cut them down, turn them into paper,
and onto them compose our beliefs,
create archives of our emptiness,
and doodle our questions to solve our griefs.

As I attempted to translate
this wonder into
a poem of pines,
onto paper, for you,

A wind blew and excited them
into waving, swinging, and swirling,
uniting them into a glorious enthusiasm
of holy roller worship that chants and sing.

And then the trees became silent,
I listened quietly, closely,
to discover that their songs never cease.
Songs for discovery, songs for inner peace.

Every cell within every pine is throbbing,
with every fibre resonating a living music,
droning and humming like harp strings,
while their incense enchants their magic.

No wonder pine groves,
and other tree groves,
were the first temples,
before they were cut down.

Bathing In The Fae's Breath

And hewn into cathedrals and churches,
that lures people further away
from the light of their guides
that we are told lead us astray.

Ailim the Pines, and their brethren trees,
see many suns rise and set,
many seasons come and go,
and many people pass by into silence.

By now
we may well wonder what
"Ogma's Tale Of The Trees"
could really be for us.

If trees had tongues
they would tell us, instead of me.
If only we had ears fine enough
to listen and trust.

Between every two pines
is a doorway
hinged to our life;
and when it has swung
open, there is
no reason to stay
silent, hidden, and
bound on the day
when we discover ... trees have tongues.

Sing away pine scented trees!
Awaken my soul to serve with ease.

some mythology of Ailim the Pine ...

I have used mythology that tells of how a Pine cannot be planted but must always find its own home. Therefore, it is said to inspire our sense of belonging, our feelings of being at home.

Bards, through the ages, have shared stories of creating personal sanctuaries where every particle of our mind, body and spirit can be at their most complete. We create sanctuaries where our vision and performance can be at their best.

about my Ailim the Pine story poem ...

When we first find ourselves in this season of life we may find ourselves feeling alone again. Also, this is the life's season when so much more seems to be very present around us. I start by expressing this through how a Pine tree grows. Pines do not respond very well to human planting. A lot of Pine plants planted by human hand do not survive, but those seeded by the elements and transported by nature seem to sow well and grow strong.

Likewise, we grow strong through our choices and not following choices of others. It is through our own planting and growing that we build our sense of belonging, and our sense of where we feel our 'spiritual' home is.

I now regret writing the line that starts with "End of a journey ..." as I do not recognize that anything comes to an end. What I am expressing is a time to pause, like the pause that happens during the change between the ebb and flow of tides.

At these times of pause, we become our most reflective. At this point of our lives, we seem to be concerned for our maturing and our ageing. One of these thoughts may be that all good times, from the vitality of being young, have gone.

So looking at the Pine, this story reveals the present that is still alive with inspirations. Every activity serves a stream of wonder as colourful as it ever was when we were children.

At this time of transition into Divine service, many people seek to follow a path through a church or Divine order.

Ailim the Pine

As this is a suite that invites people to be closer to the trees, I remind how trees were the first churches, the first altars for humans.

It is from these trees that we built churches and scribed our stories of belief and grief onto paper that was made from these trees. That is what I am doing with Ogma's Tale of The Trees too, but ....

This story turns into the distraction of the wind blowing around the Pines, followed by silence.
Each distraction seems to tune all of our senses more towards the Pine, our sight, hearing, touching, smelling, and maybe even tasting.

I move into some words from John Muir that I have altered a little. It compares our choices of cutting down trees to make churches or to be within the trees standing alive. This reflects John Muir's life, first of a Calvinist family with a lifestyle that caused him to go blind while working within a wood sawmills through to the regaining of his sight within a forest.

In a way, this story poem is calling upon people to consider the ways of John Muir as a choice of faith. Without John Muir, there may never have been forest parks, open access woodlands, the Sierra Club Friends Of The Earth, Greenpeace etc.

That is why I ask what this Ogma's Tale of The Trees could be for us. So, I finish with surreal imagery of opening the door, between two Pines, to enter into this quarter of Divine Service "on the day we discover that trees have tongues". We open the doors to leave the place where we have been 'told to be' and enter into our true Divine home to serve from.

At this fourth stage of our life, I believe we are like the Pine, as we cannot be planted by human hand, but be taken to where nature take us to feel "at home". I am sure you have noticed that "home" is a common theme through this suite.

Ohn the Gorse :

revelation

**detoxing our soul
so our visions become clearer**

*sounding the second note of the fourth aicme
second note of our Transforming Winter*

Bathing In The Fae's Breath

As a child I played in briars and gorse,
Exploring tales of ghaels, picts and norse.
Their yellow flowers always teasing,
But their prickles not so pleasing.

Gypsies gathered some, I had to inquire;
Was told they were best to ignite a fire;
To release their scent to clean the soul,
And arouse steam from their sacred bowl.

One teased me, invited me to see how they dance;
Flickering, sparking evoking a trance.
I saw more than they say a child should see;
Was told that it's all omen of who to be.

Like all people I know I went to school,
to learn, they say, or act the fool.
Reading and writing is indeed useful today,
But among the gorse I learned how to play.

some mythology of Ohn the Gorse ...

I have used mythology that tells of the Gorse being the spring cleaners of our souls.

Bards, through the ages, have shared stories of Ohn the Gorse enchanting us with its yellow flowers that are said to mirror how we react to the beauty of ourselves and of others.

The also tell us that its prickles can take us from hurt to illumination when we ignite the dry prickles that have fallen.

about my Ohn the Gorse story poem ...

This short story poem is of a childhood memory of wonder of a travelling people camped by some Gorse I was playing around by.

I watched as one lit a fire with a bunch of Gorse that flared up like a firework. My curiosity caused me to ask them what they would be doing on the fire. Their replies were very teasing, They told a string of short scary stories that scared me at first. Eventually they were stories to hear when my fear was gone.

My conclusion was there was more to learn here than the order I was being taught at school.

As an adult, I now regard those stories from the flash of Gorse on the fire are a detox that can purge our cautious misty fears and rekindle our wonder of crystal clear visions.

Bathing In The Fae's Breath

Ur the Heather :

clarity

clear vision of our quest to serve

sounding the third note of the fourth aicme
third note of our Transforming Winter

Ur the Heather

From the bonny bells of heather,
They brewed a drink long syne,
They say was far sweeter than honey,
Was stronger far than any wine.

I was born onto moorland turf,
softened by wells where summer boaters surf.
Stark moorland beauty in my vision.
Through its shrouding mist I made my decision;

To embroider my life
between the strands
of raw grasses that are
spun into this land.
Sometimes the sun briefly
ignited the folded hills,
but the mist was the life here
that watered the stills.

When summer came
into the year,
the heather bells grew
before winter crawled near.
Ready to be plucked for brewing,
they would say,
Of course, to soon
drive a cold winter away.

Bathing In The Fae's Breath

But none were alive
to tell how this elixir was made.
To find the recipe once more,
what of me must I trade?
The brewsters of the heather
are now covered in stones.
Tell me, where did their wisdom
depart from their bones.

Today the bees hum,
and the curlews cry a bitter song,
to tempt me to believe this land of heather
is not where I belong.
But once here a Pict surrendered
to a Gaelic chief,
asking please share your secret
and spare us from grief.

Aye, we could pick flower tips
of the wild purple heather;
boil them with malts and myrtle,
watch them blend together.
The floral mist and peat smoke
could bond us all in peace.
Gael and Pict have so much to share,
if we could just find the ease.

Ur the Heather

When Gaels and Picts sat close to a fire
on a cold night,
the steam from the heather ale did cool their
heated summer fight.
Steam clinged onto cold stones and dripped into
their drinking cup,
and together they cheered 'Uisge-beatha' and
united they sup.

This "water of life" they then
shared together on most days,
while they bonded the learning and wisdom
of their ways.
The fae of the heather
were pleased, of course,
that peace lasted well when
Fraoch Leann was the source.

Come thro' the heather,
around shall we gather.
Come Ronalds, come Donnells,
come all thee together,
and create drink for our
rightfu', lawfu' chief!
'Tis the heather that
now toasts our belief?

So now when we'll all go together,
maybe to pull wild mountain thyme.
Let's not forget the bloomin' heather.
Will ye go lassie go?

some mythology of Ur the Heather ...

I have used mythology that tells of Heather being an invitation to the "all seeing", a vision quest.

Bards, through the ages, have shared stories of Ur the Heather inspiring the enduring search to find the real recipe for the "water of life" to complete this quest,

They tell us that the secret is simple to find, and it is revealed through a willingness to share and encourage peace and unity under any conditions.

Ur the Heather

about my Ur the Heather story poem ...

I open the first verse of my story poem with some words, rather than lines, from Robert Burns to give the "feel" of what is to come.

With Pine, I talked of entry into this quarter of Divine Service, and with Gorse the detoxing of the soul to become clear. Here the theme should be to use this clarity of vision to serve our Divine quest.

My original story poem for this altered as, for some reason, my mind wandered into daydream visions I had on Iona and Isle of Mull in the Hebrides a long time ago.

I was, indeed, almost born onto moorland turf, but on Mull moorland turf is also abundant, so it reminded me of this too.

I would roll around and play in this bouncy turf, as I would also play and tumble in the woodland valleys too. Strangely, this is not a woodland story poem, so I omit woodland references, this time.

The moorland fires of spring and summer are mentioned, and the smoke that misted the hills. There are a few words of teasing there to lend a clue about where this story is going.

I also move on to the picking of flowers during the Heather blooming season. Flowers to brew for tea, or maybe for extractions as there are many medicines that can be made from Heather for the upcoming winter.

But what about the Heather beer that is told of in many stories? The keepers of those recipes are now buried with recipes not passed on. For a moment, I feel I should not be of these moorlands any more. I am reminded that most moorlands were once forests.

Here, I was reminded of a story on Iona telling of when Gael first met Picts. They spoke of forests, despite Iona having few trees, though legend tell of Yew trees being there centuries ago.

I end this tale of Gael and Pict chieftains sharing warm Heather ale where the steam touched the icy rocks and formed an elixir that dripped back into their mugs. This 'water of life' blessed them to unite together to serve a new wider nation. Everyone was invited to share their belief in the "water of life".

Eadha the Poplar :

transparency

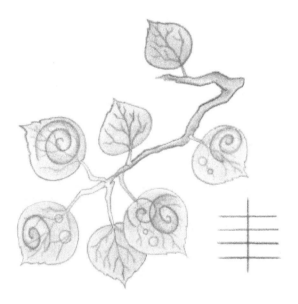

**becoming at one with all things
but owner of none**

*sounding the fourth note of the fourth aicme
fourth note of our Transforming Winter*

Bathing In The Fae's Breath

My fugitive years are all hastened away,
and I must ere long lie as lowly as they.
'Tis a sight to engage me, if anything can,
to muse on the perishing pleasures of man.

I speak of Eadha the Poplars,
felled by the woodman,
once pointed to our heavens
as far as they can,
to reveal our very small place
in the universe;
It's invitation to dance with it
to reverse our curse.

I know you, poplar.
I remember you back then.
We were introduced together,
when I was ten,
when the lonely lady on the moon
came here with scrolls,
spread her vast sleeves
and read endlessly to bleach our souls.

Eadha the Poplar

All good souls that we gathered
together were brushed,
and what we had to say about that moment
was hushed,
especially when tears came from
 an upturned bowl of rain.
I now know our task was
to soak these again and again.

At last I have adjusted
to live with day and night;
accept winter and summer
as times of dark and light.
I now dance with the universe
while other men cloy.
and now the poplar tree can only
inspire me with joy.

Since I have tuned my muse
to the trees;
voices once dim
now surround me and please.
They also gift vast silences,
to give us a place,
to be aware of what surrounds us
within each space.

The first two lines are from 'The Poplar Field' by William Cowper ...

and lines five and six from the fourth verse are translated from a poem by Chairman Mao

some mythology of Eadha the Poplar ...

I have used mythology that tells of the Poplar trunk and branches pointing to heaven to remind us to dance with all things on earth as served to us and be thankful for what we have.

Bards, through the ages, have shared stories that tell us about those who try to command the spirits of the universe upon us to spread melancholy.

They also tell us we can overcome them through dancing with all things on earth as our partners.

Opening lines are by William Cowper once a pupil at my school, then a patron who planted Poplars there.

He became an MP who passed a bill, in the 19th century, to give parents a right to excuse their children from the religious education curriculum of the school.

Eadha the Poplar

about my Eadha the Poplar story poem ...

My story poem commences with a verse from William Cowper, pronounced "cooper", revealing he was quite a "Jack The Lad" before being a school founder and parliament member (careful now).

My "I speak of Eadha the Poplars felled by the woodman" I believe is of of similar mind to Cowper's "perishing pleasures of man".

Carrying on, I touch on comparing the style of school education I was force fed into with the education I was receiving from other sources, that seemed to teach me much more.

In this story, I speak of the "lonely lady on the moon" as a metaphor for the presence of an unseen teacher that nobody seemed to be listening to anymore.

As a youngster, I thought she may be lonely, so I gathered some of my friends together to consider her wholesome 'circle spiral' approach to teaching. I think we thought that was more fun than the linear way of learning we were fed at school.

Within this story poem, I include a line of translation from Mao Tse-tung to illustrate there may be some discomfort when we change our learning choices. We need to soak ourselves into the learning of being part of all things rather than be master or owner of any of them.

I conclude by confessing that I continue to live these teachings that I was drawn to as a child. Maybe I am writing this to invite others to try out this different approach to learning.

Ioho the Yew :
wisdom

becoming attuned to cycles and resurrection, and that there is no end

sounding the fifth note of the fourth aicme
fifth note of our Transforming Winter

Bathing In The Fae's Breath

(part 1)

When the Deravid walked
through woods of old,
solemnly stalking
dressed in white and gold,
to visit and dwell
among ancient yews,
where his guide would reveal
what he needs to choose.

Pilgrims resting
in a cell,
carved in stone
by Brighid's well,
while others tramped by,
going to the fair,
joking about mirth
and the haggling they'll do there.

Bard dare to come here
once more,
to muse over mysteries
ready to pour
over these heathen types,
150% proof,
overgrown by the their diet
of gospel truth.

Ioho the Yew

(*part 2*)

Be of healthy service,
there's much for us to do
to loosen the chains
of this so called deadly yew.

Haul them away
to create happier years
that topple old time wrongs
that breed our fears;

Of being close and connected
to love and light,
that overwhelms the reign
of sin and night;

For out of darkness,
emptiness, and woe,
let's incubate happiness
to share with all we know.

Bard, dare to be called
to what is here to view
within this very intriguing tree
that renews;

Bathing In The Fae's Breath

Monster trunk,
with giant limbs of bows,
and intersecting roots,
where spirit flows.

(part 3)

The yew is said to reign
through midnight calm
o'er the bodies of those
we chose to embalm.

Unknown to us
it feeds the seed that gave us birth
from an alchemy of love,
light, and dust from this earth.

The yews that for so long
have been spared
gracing hallowed spaces
where treading is dared.

When lightnings flash
we fear tempests rage,
but we do not harm them,
we let them age.

Ioho the Yew

With stern reluctance
yews have often spoke
quivering their arms
before a woodman's stroke;

Inducing an undefined fear
of their consecrated ground
that the woodmen feel empowered
to erect fences around.

For many years
I have measured the endless steps I tread
through ancient mounds
where lay many sleeping heads;

That paid the debt of forcing nature
into dead end hallows
until their lives passed away
into these sombre shadows.

Here the young,
old, rich, the poor,
our friends, and any foes,
they all use the same door,

Servants with their masters
together lay.
The worms must feed on
all of us one day.

Bathing In The Fae's Breath

(part 4)

W.B. Yeats, When You Are Old

When you are old and grey and full of sleep,
And nodding by the fire, take down this book,
And slowly read, and dream of the soft look,
Your eyes had once, and of their shadows deep;

How many loved your moments of glad grace,
And loved your beauty with love false or true,
But one man loved the pilgrim soul in you,
And loved the sorrows of your changing face;

And bending down beside the glowing bars,
Murmur, a little sadly, how Love fled,
And paced upon the mountains overhead,
And hid his face amid a crowd of stars. (end)

Ioho the Yew

(*part 5*)

I love to retreat among the trees
away from worldly cares it's where I'm set free,
separating me from any recognition of headstones,
reminding me they'll always be life in these bones.

When will real tongues affirm the Resurrection,
instead of giving us false direction.
Belief in tenderness must become the handle
that lifts and cares, maybe gentled by a candle.

Inside the church,
stained glass casts light that's blue,
floating light that freezes us
to the cold pews.

Our hands and faces
stiffen with holiness.
Our spirits are baptized
with its starkness.

Old Yew, which graspest at the stones
That name the under-lying dead.
Thy fibres net the dreamless head.
Thy roots are wrapt about the bones.

Bathing In The Fae's Breath

Nay, Traveller! do rest here.
This lonely yew-tree stands
Far from all human dwelling.
What if here the bee love
not these barren boughs?

(part 6)

Who, through any silent hour
of inward thought,
can revere lowliness of heart,
it must be thwart.

Bard, this Yew connects all you are,
all you seek.
No openings, no conclusions,
no! no! this is not weak.

Yes, you can always
be evergreen;
Always be part of all
you have seen;

Solid and dependable
as nature made you;
Wise bard, connecting with all
like the regenerating Yew.

Ioho the Yew

I will leave you now
but as I leave I also return.
I can never serve you
all you will learn.

But I can give you all I have
through voice and script
as we are bonded friends
in this life and into the next.

Where Beith the Birch
is the first life on this earth
born here from another world, they say.

From this first birch
all trees,
all plants,
all animals
and ourselves , were served the first breath of life.

And Ogma's Tale Of The Trees ...
is told once more ...

Verses 20, 21 and 22, are 'When You Are Old' by W.B. Yeats, Verse 27 is from 'Old Yew' a poem by Alfred Tennyson , Verse 28 and the first two lines of verse 29 are from 'Lines Left Upon A Seat' by William Wordsworth.

some mythology of Ioho the Yew ...

I have used mythology that tells of the Yew being about the End, but also tells of the Yew being of the Resurrection.

Bards, through the ages, have shared stories of Ioho the Yew being an arouser of the dark side of spirits, and our fear. They tell tales about Yew roots weaving through the skulls of corpses of those fallen who's life has passed on.

They tell us of the Yew being the bringer of transformation and resurrection, as the Yew is a tree that continually re-births itself from within.

Like the Yew, my story poem completes a cycle while beginning another as a never ending spiral; perhaps proving there is a lot we can learn from the rings of a tree trunk.

Ioho the Yew

about my Ioho the Yew story poem ...

This longest, and, perhaps, most complex of my twenty story poems of Ogma's Tale Of The Trees returns to the Deravid again. I introduced the Deravid through my Fearn The Alder story poem.

Some folks call themselves Druids or the Drui, today. To me, many seem to adorn this title to position themselves as heads of something, such as an Order maybe?

A modern church is built to serve as a gathering place of an Order too. To me, the adornment a druid chooses to wear can be an attempt to follow an Order tradition. Order takes us from Nature to be something else.

So where has this tradition has come from? Old literature and old photos give clues, maybe? What about the interpretations through television shows and movies.

My approach is not to judge the faith of the people that I call Deravids here. I believe they are trying to find their "way", like all of us, as teachers teaching what they need to know.

Whoever he is, and however he is, this Deravid dwells among the ancient Yews believing his spirit guide I will reveal what he needs to know. Yes, he is a "he" for very good reason here.

Next verse throws in a comparison of extremes. I feature silent people in retreat within a stone cell while passing by near them is an extreme of noisy jolly people going off to the fair.

The stone imagery among the silent people is very important here as it includes stone images carved by human hand.

At this point, I ask why do we need silence and meditation. Why not just drop "everything", call some friends, get social with each other, have some fun and "go with the flow"?

Through the third verse, the Deravid is now speaking. I think we can now assume this is Ogma. Here he is making a judgement, as he measures the revellers against the retreaters.

Continuing into the next verse he mentions "Chains of this so called deadly Yew?". What is unraveling here? Ogma is requesting that we serve healthier service.

Instead of commanding Order that has driven people into fear of committing "old time wrongs", how about letting our pure inspired conscience guide the way we live?

Ogma the Deravid goes on to explain this as letting "love and light" overcoming "sin and night". Night here being a symbol of darkness, of course. The Deravid then calls the Bard to closely view the Yew as "this very intriguing tree that renews".

For many people, the Yew tree is a symbolic tree within cemeteries, the last resting place where lifeless embalmed bodies are buried and eventually decay. A Yew may be regarded as a guarding a place of death, the end of our lives, especially as itself is a very toxic tree, but is it?

Eventually, the worms will feed on these buried bodies and transform them from their human form into food that feeds other new life.

The Yew is not like other trees that lives a life and dies. From the centre of the Yew, its trunk is constantly renewing itself with new vibrant young wood that grows outwards and ages over the years.

When we visit cemeteries, we may fill our thoughts with images of our herocs lost and buried under stones. What if we thought of those heroes letting go of who they were. By doing so, does this release new spirit of life to feed new seeds that sprout and be born?

Have you seen green cemeteries? These beautiful new cemeteries are reverence towards a belief in renewal rather than complete death. Where a fallen body lays, a buried body's flesh and spirit is allowed to be free and feed into a new tree that grows in its place. Reverence to a living tree replaces reverence to a lifeless stone.

Eventually, I take the poem away from the Deravid and ask how we really approach living. Do we try to control living from birth to death to ensure we follow a linear path? Do we accept life as a cycle of cycles while we are alive within our human bodies, and beyond when our body is done?

I flow the story into thoughts about how, in the same cemetery, the young and old, rich and poor, masters and servants all lay together, and how all of their spirits go through the same door.

Then comes the words of the W.B. Yeats poem, "When We Are Old".

Ioho the Yew

After this is the finale of the spiral of the entire Ogma's Tale Of The Trees.

Here I complete the tale's 360 degrees before the story spiral continues on into another spiral orbit. For a moment, the veil of the entire cycle opens up all together

I say why I love to retreat among the trees.
I ask when the Resurrection will be firmly affirmed
I provoke the cold and starkness that some people feel through the faith they are told to follow.

I quote a verse from Tennyson who's poem of the Yew fixates on the Yew being of our End

I follow that with a verse from Wordsworth who seems to speak of the Yew as a regenerating passing

"What if here the bee love not these barren boughs?" where would our lives be, where would all lives be?

The overall theme of this Ogma's Tale Of The Trees is then revealed.

Bathing In The Fae's Breath

Yes, you, me, everyone, we can all be bards, all be evergreen, dependable as Nature made us, to connect with all things.

Nobody can ever teach or serve us what we learn, but everyone can serve what they have, and hat they know, so others may be inspired.

My thought here is that every teacher only teaches what the teacher needs to learn ... and this is what bonds us from this world and into the next where Beith The Birch is the first life on this earth.

Through this entire work I ask -
Find The Bard within yourself,
do not let anyone try to take that away from you, because this is of life itself, as Nature intended.

Now off I go to do some
Bathing In The Fae's Breath:-)
You are invited to share this with me too,
if you wish. See a later chapter.

Find Your Story :

at Carrowcrory,
or at your venue too,

'Find Your Story'

**retreat workshop
guided by Woodland Bard**

worldwide inquiries welcome

- one day, two days, three days, five days, seven days
- various curriculums and itineraries
- retreat accommodation available for up to 18 people

from inspiration to voice

Do you ever ask, "how can I find my voice"
or even "where can I find an audience"?

You may feel a calling to express yourself through writing, filming, painting, composing, performing.

**Let us help you to find your voice
... then find your audience.**

Find Your Story – origins

'Find Your Story' is an invitation to release your 'old snake skin' through embracing inspiration, nurturing your spirit, and sharing it through the 'voice' of your natural art.

This workshop activity and it's title came about totally unexpected, and unplanned ...

Claire Roche had a thatched cottage restored here at Carrowcrory, Co. Sligo, Ireland, and I planted a Tree Labyrinth, in response to multiple dreams about it. Now, several visiting groups have used it.

Each year, the trees in this Tree labyrinth have grown well and it has become a small woodland with native trees, herbs, some flowers, and there is still a labyrinth path to walk. It is slowly becoming a permaculture garden that will soon be a forest foods and herbal woodland.

A woodland labyrinth session here at Carrowcrory is followed by a happy tea and scones session. This is followed by stories, songs, harps and poems around the turf fire hearth.

What happened to the people, who walked the labyrinth, surprised themselves and surprised us too.

Most visitors here have never walked a labyrinth before. They usually enter our Tree Labyrinth with some sense of caution and trepidation, but also with excited anticipating curiosity.

... and they leave this labyrinth with faces glowing.

As we shared tea and scones, each person had a wonderful story to share, purely from revealing inspirations they allowed themselves to receive and nurture while walking through the labyrinth.

So, I wondered if there was a way we could share the opportunity for others to enjoy this experience, at other places away from our Tree Labyrinth here at Carrowcrory?

Shall we go on tour, and invite people to join us who cannot visit our Tree Labyrinth in Ireland? ...

Find Your Story – on tour, anywhere!

To replicate this experience elsewhere, I needed to do this without dependence on having a tree or plant based labyrinth available? - yet be surrounded by Nature. I have discovered this is a workshop that can work very well in many forest, botanical and herbal environments :-)

Being an Ireland interpretation of this 'inspiration to story experience', it is somewhat connected to what people call Celtic mythology. Therefore, there 'has' to be ... the essential **'three steps'** to doing this, such as three stages of labyrinth walking, and three stages of 'Finding Your Story'.

For a labyrinth guide or facilitator, these steps are often called the classical names of
 'purgation', 'illumination' and 'unity'.

- A life coach may name these steps as 'challenges', 'choices', and 'outcomes'.
- A herbalist may say, describe these as 'condition', 'nourishment', and 'healing'.
- A storyteller may describe these as
 'being present', 'trusting inspiration',
 let inspiration be your voice'.

Landscapes That Open

First step is about 'releasing baggage'.

Landscapes around people, in any place, seem to define their challenges, guilt, concerns, fear, and anxieties. Change a landscape around a person and see how they change.

I know I feel as if I am a different human here in rural Carrowcrory to the person I am in Dublin city. It's not about good or bad ... just different.

First step is enter into a landscape that encourages our mind, body and spirit to become present.

We trust the 'purgation' of 'unwanted baggage' that is bonded to us. As I use mythology imagery to describe things, I call this experience 'the shedding of our old snake skin'.

My favourite tools for doing this 'purgation' are a walk in a forest or walking through a living labyrinth of trees, herbs, flowers or hedges.

Being present among fragrant herbs,
is another option ...

There are spaces where entering the free outdoors is very restricted. If so, I find this is best through using the actual raw plant material of herbs rather than from preparations made from them.

For example, I prefer a lighted sage or lavender smudging stick than burning sage or lavender oil.

In every situation, it is best to use and appreciate what we have access to rather than have a longing for what is not present. So, we use what we have living around us.

Light That Blossoms

The next step is about 'light'.

Many people define this through converting 'light' into an image that they may call their Christ, Angel, Spirit Guide, Goddess, God, Animal Guide, Invisible Friend or another image.

It is light that's not visible, but we know it is there. We still 'see' it and sense it in some way.

Again I come up with mythology and call this 'Sí de Óg' (shee d-owg), unseen Presence Of Love.

People who join us with this experience give this light names, usually feminine names. Some people discover they feel 'called to' Divine guiding work that assists people to recognize and embrace this light, live with it, and walk with it.

Some of these people have the courage to call themselves 'Light Workers'. Others call themselves 'Priests', 'Shamans', and 'Ministers'.

I address all of these personal 'light' images with the words **'The Presence Of Love'**, which, so far, seems to be accepted by everyone present on these workshops. I feel this nicely describes the starting point of what their images are about.

The Story Grows

The third step is engaging with this 'love', this 'light', this 'nourishment' and accept and embrace what reveals itself as a sequence of images.

... and this is what become **'Your Story'**.

It is like a sensory miracle where the life of our five senses seems to meet in a central womb and synthesizes into an incubated dream.

This dream grows into a clarity you can understand, and can describe. So, with your encouragement, your acceptance, and love, it keeps growing.

'Your Story' instantly becomes a story to share, to tell to an 'audience' through your chosen medium of expression.

Classically, you may believe this expression deserves to be shared through writing a book, composing music and songs and recording a disc, or maybe revealing images through painting,

You may feel urged to translate this imagery through a performing art such as drama, dance and mime, to explore its meaning and purpose.

Primitively, this expression would have been shared through oral storytelling traditions.

And is Harvested and Shared

When **'Your Story'** gives birth, it is fresh fruit. It deserves consumption when fresh. This is when it is at it's most nourishing and most life-giving, when listened to.

Today, the freshest expression and sharing is through digital mediums. We now have rapid worldwide distribution through services such as ...

- journal blogs - through services like Google Blogger and Wordpress,
- audio distribution - through services such as Soundcloud and Podbean,
- video distribution - through YouTube, Vimeo, and Facebook

The fresh harvest content we distribute through these services can also blend and synthesize into multimedia e-books.

Your content can be stored for careful preservation and maturing like any abundant harvest.

By this, I mean editing **'Your Story'** into beautiful archives of printed books and recorded discs, that millions of people still enjoy today. And people will enjoy for many more years yet.

may I invite you to join a Find Your Story Workshop?

I provide links in my last chapter here, **'Encore'**.

Be A Bard In The Woods :

In Ireland, we host a series of Bards In The Woods meet-ups within Public Forests around Ireland. We gather together on Sunday afternoons between the first week of March, which is also National Tree Week here, and last week of October.

Our meet ups tend to go through four stages.

Nature Walk, Foraging, Quiet Time, Bard Time, Shared picnic.

The **Nature Walk** is a very social time. We have just met up, excited about being in the woods together and while there help each other with identification of trees and plants. We may talk about sustainable foraging and how to make oils, tinctures, poultices, teas, and salves at home.

Using the 'Find Your Story' trinity, this is indeed the 'purgation' time.

When we have settled down and walked a bit we tend to settle into a **Quiet Time**. Some people may describe this time as Forest Therapy, Forest Mindfulness, Forest Bathing, Shinrin Yoku, or my favourite, Boladh na Sióga.

There is a lot of science bantered about explaining how exposure to natural environments improve our well being and protect us from serious health. A lot of what we call Aromatherapy has come from essential oils that trees and plant emit into the forest air.

I saw this list of 8 Proven Benefits somewhere. Personal experience seems to verify much of this...

- Boosts immune system
- Lowers blood pressure
- Reduces stress
- Improves mood
- Increases ability to focus
- Accelerates recovery from surgery or illness
- Increases energy level
- Improves sleep

Rather than think of a cure, which is very linear, I like to encourage people present to consider their senses. This is an expanded 'stop and smell the roses' invitation.

Using the 'Find Your Story' trinity, this is indeed the 'illumination' time.

It is fun, inspiring, and revealing, when we pay attention to what we see, hear, touch, smell, and taste. Yes, 'taste' as we do taste what is in the air in the forest if we pay attention to this for a moment.

Some of the people who join us have been to Forest Bathing, Mindfulness, Yoga, Meditation and Reiki schools so they like to share and try out their skills, such as guided meditations and coached therapy.

Other people with us like break out and go off to be alone, maybe to write. Others like to be in a quiet group to share silence together. This stage is very freewill.

Next, we go onto our favourite Bardic Spot for our **Bard Time**. I can relate this to the third stage of the 'Find Your Story' trinity, the 'unity' time.

Sometimes we need to tell everyone to meet there at a certain time if everyone breaks away. A Bardic Spot is often an old heritage tree near water.

This is the space to share our favourite poems or stories here, which may be our own. We encourage everyone to have a go if they can.

Bathing In The Fae's Breath

I try not to put any controls on this, but the enthusiastic ones can easily drift on into 20 minutes, 30 minutes or more of reciting their stuff.

I suggest about 5 minutes per person. With some people, this is 3 or 4 or their one minute poems, while others may need to just give excerpts from their epics.

The 'space' at this point is to allow everyone to share 'their voice' without any intimidation. This is why we encourage these events to be in 'Public Forests' because we are the owners.

I receive several requests asking 'please do Bards In The Woods in my woods'. This is very kind, and we do take up these offers sometimes.

As kind as the offer is, and no matter how warm the host is, there is still that lingering intimidation from having an 'owner' present and being on 'owned' land.

The other essential benefit from this Bardic Time is each presenter has a very attentive audience. The combination of 'finding your voice' and having an 'audience to listen to that voice' is very fulfilling well being nutrition.

Confidence is raised. During this time I personally believe in 'Trust In The Fae'.

So, after all that, we retire to our **Shared Picnic,** and an incredible celebration that becomes.

We try to support local foods with what we bring along, but there is no 'whip cracking' with that. The sharing of anything we can bring to the picnic table is good.

Sometimes, we cannot bring anything, and that includes accidently leaving food at home. It does not matter as there is always plenty to share. Just bring twice as much next time :-). There are no rules for this, just suggestions.

During these picnics, we really open up to each other and have a lot of fun. Obviously there is a lot of talk about gardening, local food hubs and recipes during this time, as well as talk about families ... and a bit of native, natural human gossip too.

Bards In The Woods is much more than, perhaps, a clinical Forest Therapy session. All four stages of our meet up assist our well being.

The fun and banter while we share plant lore is just as essential as reflective sensual quiet time.

Voice and audience commune through our Bardic words, and fellowship we share during our picnics all adds towards a revitalizing wholesome session. It helps us feel good through the week ahead

Perhaps you can try this for yourselves?

If you are in Ireland on Sundays, I hope you may join us for our Bards In The Woods.
See the Encore last chapter page for links.

Be A Bard In The Woods

Sleeping Awake :

I have kept this poem for this place because I feel these few words sum up my entire book here.

It is a Rite Of Passage thought; a sunset of our waking life on earth that is followed by another sunrise somewhere.

This echoes my passion living a circular spiral vision life rather than linear life. By doing so I believe we are on the same 'wave' as the rest of Nature. Nothing in Nature needs calibrations for time and distance to map their lives.

Visually, this is also reflecting what I mentioned in another chapter about 'green burials' instead of 'stone burials' ...

Sleeping Awake

When my spirit departs from my body,
it will rejoin the river of spirit that flows
not to any particular place,
but to all places at the same time.

My body will rejoin the earth
and commune as one, once again.

A tree will be born from where my body faded,
and melted from its unique singular vessel
into an acceptance of letting go,
no longer protecting what it does not own

What was 'my' temple
will nourish another body again.

The tree grows, holding and caring for
another singular droplet of spirit,
separated from that timeless river,
to guide the tree into reaching out and sharing.

From that tree another living temple being
will be nourished again.

The dance of dreaming and joy continues ...

Encore :

Again, thank you for browsing my
'Bathing In The Fae's Breath' book here.

To explore more of what we do, such as visiting us here in Ireland or inviting us to visit you, these links should interest you.

- My **Woodland Bard** pages are here ...
  woodlandbard.com

- **Bathing In The Fae's Breath** here ...
  faesbreath.com

- **Ogma's Tale Of The Trees** pages here ...
  ogmatrees.com

- **Bards In The Woods** here ...
  bardsinthewoods.com

Afternoon at Carrowcrory Cottage ...

Carrowcrory Cottage is a restored traditional cottage with a reed thatched roof and walls built with rubble stone and bog oak lintels. The floors are blue limestone and, yes, we do have a turf fire.

The garden area is a tree and herb labyrinth with a 400 metre meditative labyrinth walk path. It includes a live Willow entrance, tunnel, and central cairn.

We introduce what we do here, by arrangement, between 2 pm and 5 pm during an afternoon.

- introduction to local Irish tree lore
- an adventure using our Tree Labyrinth,
- afternoon tea and scones with storytelling
- songs, poems and harps around the hearth

When everyone gathers for tea and scones, after their labyrinth time, we invite our guests to share inspirations that came to them in the labyrinth, with the help of a '**talking stick**'.

The person with the stick is the 'voice' and everyone else is the 'audience'. It's remarkable what stories people are inspired to tell after just a short introductory walk in this labyrinth.

We complete the afternoon with some songs and stories from singer harpist **Claire Roche** around the hearth.

Though the harp is the symbol of Ireland very few people visiting Ireland actually see anyone perform with a harp.

This 'session' includes a poem or two from me, and most important, anyone else present can add and share a song or poem with us at this time.

This afternoon is for groups of any size, from 2 people to 24 people, and must be pre-booked to ensure both Claire and I are available for you.

Encore

We can arrange local accommodation if you are staying in the area the night before, the night after, or even longer, as there is plenty to see and do around here.

To complete your day here, we suggest a morning visiting our local Spring Well and a walk up to our local Céis Caves that are full of local lore. We can arrange excellent light lunches at the local Fox's Den pub. The family there brew their own White Hag ales, including Heather Ale, worth trying.

If you stay in the area longer we are close to Carrowkeel Cairns, Moytura with ancient sites. These include Labby Rock and Heapstown Cairn (Well Of Slaine), Lough Meelagh with the Knockranny Court Cairn and other sites, Boyle with Abbey with Sheela na gig and other nearby sites, ... and I could keep adding to this list.

Plenty to do around here if you stayed
2, 3, 5, 7, 10 or even 14 days.

To enjoy an ...'Afternoon at Carrowcrory Cottage', or longer, and make arrangements with us, please visit our '**Carrowcrory Cottage**' web site ...
carrowcrorycottage.com

Bathing In The Fae's Breath

Dedications and thanks to many ...

There is the famous well worn proverb that 'behind every successful man is a good woman'.

Success for me, right now,
is getting this book out to you.

... and that one 'good women' that motivated this work and supported me throughout deserves me dedicating this to her ... my singer harper love Claire Roche, often the 'Fae's Breath' herself. :-)

Many thanks also for the ongoing wonder and inspiration of my adult children, Jamie, Sky, Holly, Ivy who live and have lived terrific lives as well as share their lives with incredible spouses and their close friends, who also inspire me too.

Thanks to those who were friends with me in child years and through grammar school years who are still alive, fit and seem to remember more about me as a young 'un than I remember myself.

Thanks to my father, though very distant and rarely seen, was of a family of true sacred wisdom that I am proud to have been descended from.

Special mention for my father's brother, my Uncle Cecil. He kept me in bikes and sometimes cycled with me to ancient sites where he picked up Hazel or Willow rods and be the diviner in residence.

Thanks to my mother. Though she passed on when I was a wee 4 years old, her spirit has lived on and guided me well.

Thanks to my first stepmother, though a bitter relationship she was fiercely motivating. It was her who assertively encouraged me to read quickly, got me to perform on stage and improvise, and face fear head on from a very early age.

Special thank you to ....
Milena Rooney of Spiral Path Designs
who served the beautiful illustrated art for the Ogma's Tale Of The Trees section on this book

Thanks to present friends. They know who they are, but If I start naming them someone will be left out, but thanks to all of you for constantly cheering me on.

Huge thanks and hugs to the many people who invested in the initial cost of making this book and accompanying music CD possible.

Dedications

Thanks to 1000s of people who told me stories that entered here, Attie McKechnie, Father Finan, Robin Williamson, Kate Corkery and 100s of foresters. fishermen and farmers come to mind.

Photo pics in this book are mainly my own, some antique public domain pics and a couple of modern public domain pics. Thank you wonderful Bards In The Woods people, Bridget Foy, Charlie Easterfield, Jane Gilgun, Blue Germein, Jan McEnvoy, Andy Beach, Denise O'Toole, Bee Smith, Tony Cuckson, Erika Schowalter Rae, who are in pics here.

No citation list here as credits are given through the book. Barely any books or articles were referred to for this book. The content of this book is mainly my responses to storytellers, paintings, and landscapes.

And back to Claire Roche, who constantly encourages that what I write actually means something. Then when she adds her harps to the words, the magic is spun ...

Bathing In The Fae's Breath

Thank you all for joining me here with ...
'Bathing In The Fae's Breath'.

Woodland Bard
x x x

Made in the USA
Monee, IL
13 August 2022